WHO CONTROLS?

By Ardyce C. Whalen

The essays herein are on topics that greatly concern me. I am the mother of five children, with children of their own. I worry about the kind of lives they'll have. I was also a teacher of junior and senior high students while my children were growing up, and I know how confusing the teen years can be—for two months, until a birthday came along, I had five teenagers. The world back then was no picnic, but it seems more messed up now it was then. When we should have been stewards of our Earth, we have to often been destroyers. We haven't been good to each other either. We've made great advances in areas such as medicine and technology, but in other areas, such as basic human rights, we seem to have regressed. We are stuck in a "King of the Hill" mentality.

Dedicated to the memory of
Margaret Sanger

Who Controls?

Table of Contents

Who Controls?

Introduction

I wiggled a bit, trying to get comfortable on the wooden seat of the high-backed booth of the café. I chose a dimly lit corner, as I wanted privacy. Outside it rained, inside it was chilly, and I sighed with content as I wrapped my hands around a steaming cup of coffee, to warm my cold fingers. I faced the back wall of the café; I didn't want to see people entering, but I could hear them. Just then a couple settled into the booth in front of me, the man sharing the other side of my booth's back. They began talking.

It was hard to hear the woman; she must have sat across from the man, and her voice was low, but I did hear her say, "What's with men?" and then, "That subject was settled decades ago," followed by "That's just so mean spirited!"

I tried not to listen, really I did, but the man's voice came across loud and clear as he said, "Hey, that's my kid you're carrying! He's got half my genes. You got to cherish him. When that kid comes, *he's* your job."

She raised her voice a bit to protest, "You're kidding, right? I love my job…good money, though not as much as if I was a man, but they're talking about equal pay for equal work."

"I know, I know. Our Declaration of Independence says 'All men are created equal,' and some say that includes women. Women are considered men in that instance, but nobody really believes it. Men with wombs! The thought makes me sick. I say that if the founding fathers, all smart guys, had meant women too, they would have written, '*All men and women are created equal*,' but they didn't.

"Tough luck, Sister, but that womb thing is a BIG THING-- too big for girls unless we control it, and we can only do that by controlling you females. To HELL with Planned Parenthood! We deserve to be in control of production. We're the ones who gets it all started, so don't let me catch you sneaking out to some female-run agency that allows you to decide what's best. *I* know what's best for you.

"What's that? You say you have a mind and can make your own decisions? What planet are you living on? Men are in control. The world is a "pa-tri-arch-y." You know what that is, don't you, Honey? If it ever was a matriarchy, which I doubt, those days are long gone.

"The biggest mistake we made was giving your gals the right to vote. Now you are 53% of all voters in America! It's not our fault you got a womb that carries our seed--OUR SEED! Be careful with it, for it's that ability that makes you valuable. We'd get rid of you but for that. Well, maybe not. Sex if fun, especially if it's with someone young and pretty and you sure fit the bill, Baby!

"Even you should be able to understand why we need to put the screws on now. You-all are just getting too big for your panties. We need to dial it back to the glorious 50's, to the days of Beaver Cleaver with a mom in an apron.

"So what if the world is overpopulated? There's just too many of *them*, not us. Those other countries can thin themselves out by wars and famines. 'Out of sight, out of mind,' that's my motto.

"Speaking of mind, all the "mind" you need, Sweetie, is a mind to "mind" our children. It's what nature intended."

"Hey, where are you going? I'm not done yet!"
I heard her footsteps moving fast and furious on the wooden floor and then the sound of a door closing. Stunned, I thought over what I'd heard; I couldn't believe it. Perhaps it never really happened. I daydream a lot, could I have imagined…? No, someone must have told me…or did I read it in a novel? In any case, it was a snapshot of what is going on in America these days—the so-called "War on Woman."

Who Controls?

Much has been made recently of the so-called War on Women taking place in our nation's Congress and in the governments of many states. Battles are being waged to wrest control of reproduction away from women, fights women thought had been won with the advent of the Pill and the ruling in Roe v. Wade in 1973. They were wrong.

Fear is at the heart of it all, just as it was back in the mid-nineteenth century and early twentieth century when immigrants poured into the United States. At that time, the West was open to settlement, and Yankees were determined that it not be settled by the Irish, Poles, Scandinavians, Slavs, and such like; these people would get too much political clout. White men were in a panic, but what could they do about it? They'd enlist the women by passing laws against birth control and abortion; thereby, literally forcing women into maternity in an effort to outnumber less desirable, in their eyes, the people flooding onto our shores.

Information about contraception was considered obscene and prohibited by the Comstock Act of 1873, an act against distribution of any obscene material through the mail. Many states passed similar laws, referred to collectively as the Comstock Laws. Sometimes the states' laws outlawed both the use and also the distribution of contraceptives.

The earliest laws against abortion were laws against the commercialization of abortion producing plants. But the push was on, and by 1880 every state had criminalized abortion, with the exception of therapeutic abortion to save a woman's life.

Today, white men are again in a panic for fear of becoming outnumbered in the United States by Hispanics, blacks, Asians, and Native Americans, who will by 2050 make up about 54% of our country's population (US census). With minority status comes loss of political power—my G-d we've already got a black President! What to do? They decide, consciously or subconsciously, to enlist the aid of white women.

Women, however, fight the proposed strictures on contraception and abortion. They've tasted the freedom that comes with control of reproduction, of having a life beyond diapers and parent-teacher meetings. They're becoming doctors, and lawyers, and such: Forced Maternity? No way.

Fear of the "invasion of the immigrants" has again raised its ugly head, this time; women will refuse to passively knuckle under.

Earth: Our Beautiful Mother

We have a beautiful
mother
Her green lap
immense
Her brown embrace
eternal
Her blue body
everything
we know.

--by Alice Walker (1991)

James B. Irwin, of *Apollo 15*, marveled at the beauty of our mother as he looked down upon Earth from far out in space. He stated that it looked like a marble, "the most beautiful you can imagine. That beautiful, warm, living object looked so fragile, so delicate, that if you touched it with a finger it would crumble and fall apart."

But it is not the Earth itself that is fragile; we are the fragile ones, the vulnerable ones, though we imagine ourselves to be ever exempt from the natural laws that apply to all other life forms. Though we deny it, the umbilical cord is still intact. We are our mother's dependents, as are all life forms on Earth.

Nor is the Earth beautiful and warm, as in the sense of being loving and caring. We have changed all that in our desire to "subdue" our mother. A close up view reveals that much of the Earth is full of ugliness, with continual wars, polluted air and water, deforestation, and strip-mining, to name a few of the abominations created by fear and greed. The careless, heavy-handed way in which we humans treat the Earth, other life forms, and each other shall demand a day of reckoning, a day that may be sooner than we think. As for the Earth being warm, isn't it getting a bit *too* warm? What about the number and severity of tornadoes these days? Could it be that our mother is becoming angry?

We can, if we lose our attitude, our arrogance, build a safe and humane world while living within natural laws. Picture a world in which children need not go to bed hungry, a world in which they are not blown apart or shot at, a world in which education and health care is available to all; a world in which trees, clean air, and sufficient water abound. It sounds like "pie in the sky," but we can bring this scenario down to Earth.

A serious impediment to creating a better world is our amazing fertility. We forget that nature has a way of dealing with a species that becomes too plentiful. Woman has always been more in tune with nature than has man; woman, the producer of new life, could save the day. In fact, she could save all our days to come, if she is given the chance. It all has to do with choice and the answer to an old question: Which is best, *quantity* or *quality*?

In the past, man, as in the male of the species, has usually chosen *quantity* of children so he'd have help in the fields, sons to inherit, and a way for his characteristics to live on after his death— a kind of tangible immortality. Woman, on the other hand, usually wants *quality*.

Implicit in this choice is fewer children; nine months of pregnancy and years of childcare undoubtedly influence her choice.

Historically, when fewer children lived to make it to maturity, the man's choice made sense. Today, humans fill the Earth, using up her resources at an alarming rate, killing each other over the possession of these resources and of territory. On October 31, 2011, the world's population reached seven billion. The United Nations (CNN) predicts that the world population will number 9.1 billion by 2050. This large a number cannot help but negatively affect our quality of life.

We have been given big brains; let's use them. It is clearly time for woman to have her way, time for quality to trump quantity, but she can't do it alone.

Who Controls?

All nations must help their women to take control of their bodies' reproductive capacity. The result would be fewer babies, as she puts quality before quantity. Planet Earth needs fewer footprints in the sand or anywhere else.

Conclusion

If we continue producing children willy-nilly we will bring into the world more disease, more poverty, more wars, and more destruction of our Earth and her resources. So many of these problems would be lessened or solved if we decreased our numbers. We can do it; we have the know-how, all we need is the will power.

James B. Irwin looked down upon our Earth and it appeared to him as a beautiful, warm, delicate marble. He did not see the ugliness of war and pollution from out in space. We can eliminate the dissonance between the two views. If we strive for quality, rather than quantity, Earth, our only home, can be truly beautiful with room for all

Who Controls?

From Breadwinner to Loser

In mists of time the male would hunt
The giant deer and mastodon.
With bloody meat at her feet,
A grateful woman gave him some.

He claims the land crops grow upon.
A sweaty farmer he becomes.
His house, his wife, enrich his life
To earn her keep, she'll give him sons.

A lonely mom, no sisters nigh
To give her aid when babies cry.
A thrall; that's all she'll ever be.
Freedom trumped by security.

The first of our species began to walk upright about 3 to 3.5 million years ago ("Science of the Sexes: 2. Different by Design"). At some undetermined time during this long span of years, the female of the species ceased to go into estrus and began to menstruate. Estrus had made for a wild, happy meeting of the minds and bodies, but the advent of menstruation had the opposite effect. It injected uncertainty into sexual relations. A man never knew when a woman was ovulating; most of the time, the woman didn't know either.

Males and females both wanted sex, it is one of the basic needs along with food and water, but males wanted it more strongly than did females. After menstruation replaced estrus, females figured out that sex and pregnancy went together, and that pregnancy often meant death. That is a strong reason to say "No!" to a sexually aroused male. Dr. Shlain believes that when humans began to walk upright, their bodies began to change. The spine became perpendicular and the pelvis "scrunched" together. In addition, babies' heads were getting bigger, resulting in a high frequency of childbirth deaths, especially among the youngest females; hence the fear of pregnancy (Shlain 4-5).[1] Females whose sex drive overrode their fears would die in greater numbers than those females with stronger will power. In time, females with weaker sex drives and stronger wills would be in the majority. Paradoxically, as woman's sex drive weakened, man's sex drive became "turbo charged" (Shaun's term). This made for confusion and conflict; the so-called "battle of the sexes" began.

If things had stopped there, the battle between male and female might have ended the human race, but menstruation, in addition to bringing disharmony to sexual relations, also evened the playing field by making woman as dependent on man as man was on woman. During menstruation, a woman lost fairly large amounts of iron-rich blood each month. Child bearing occasioned even more blood loss, and the subsequent lactation robbed her body of additional iron. She needed to replace the iron, and the best way to do this was by eating meat—vegetable iron was just too difficult to digest (Shlain, 5-36). She needed a brave hunter to kill game for her; and he, with his powerful sex drive, needed sex. "Candy may be dandy," and "liquor quicker" but red meat was a shoo-in.

While the men hunted, the women and children set out with digging sticks to find edible vegetable matter. The women's efforts provided close to 80 percent of the food for the tribe ("Science of the Sexes"). The 20 percent contributed by the hunters must not be underestimated because it was crucial; not only to the health of the women, but to the health of the men's sex lives. Men wanted women for sex and women needed iron-rich meat to replace iron lost through childbirth and lactation.

The skills of both sexes were needed to provide food in sufficient quantity and variety; "Man became the "meatwinner," and woman became the breadwinner" (Morgan 161). Though it was a division of labor, it was also a partnership of equals. Morgan sees this division of labor as the start of the nuclear family (203).

Who Controls?

Approximately 40,000 years ago, according to records around the world, burials and "grave goods" came into existence, indications that Homo sapiens were aware of death, and the males, in particular, were fearful.[2] At about the same time, males became aware of their paternity. In the awareness of paternity, lay a partial easement of the males "death fear"; if he had children, a part of him could still exist even though he was in his grave (Shlain, 271-299).

There was only one problem: he had to be certain that the children were really his. One way of insuring this was to marry a virgin, but he also wanted to have sex whenever he could with all women. [Things haven't changed much as evidenced by the popularity of the bumper sticker; SO MANY WOMEN SO LITTLE TIME.] If other men wanted the same thing, he couldn't be sure that ALL his children were really his. He'd have to make a pact with other men that they'd not have sex with another man's woman. Women were in favor of such a pact, because it meant that they would have help in raising their children, and they would have a protector. This pact morphed into the marriage ceremony (Shlain 271-299).

> Marriage, therefore, came out of man's desire to legitimize his heirs, and woman's desire to have help in the raising of children—to be provided for and protected. The actual CEREMONY came into being because it would bind them together in the eyes of their peers, thus making for a stronger union. (Shlain, 307-31)

The ceremony was meant to bind them until death, though if the woman was barren or lacking in some significant way, however, the man could "put her away from him" (Morgan 210).

Marriage had advantages for both sexes. Men's fear of death lessened, and women had help and protection during child rearing. Men continued to hunt and women and children continued to gather. A cultural revolution, however, was soon to occur and it would change everything.

The revolution was agriculture. Domestication of animals first occurred about 12,000 years ago with, most likely, the dog. Plant domestication is about 10,000 years old, but people did not depend on domesticated animals or plants until around 6,000 years ago ("Sustainability"). So until around 6,000 years ago, Homo sapiens depended mainly on hunting and gathering to live.

The advent of agriculture was one giant step forward for man, but many steps backward for woman. The balance of power between man and woman was utterly destroyed. Man was the master; woman, robbed of her female support system, was the slave. It was a divide-and-conquer strategy, and it worked.

You might argue that woman was a slave before: a slave to her body's need for red meat, but at that time, man was equally her slave because of his need for sex. Though not always harmonious, their relationship was that of equals.

You might also argue that woman was a slave to the unwieldiness of her body during pregnancy and to the demands of motherhood. You'd have a point, but she had the help of her daughters, her sisters, the other women of the tribe, and the older children of the tribe. She was not alone and unprotected; she had a strong female support system.

When man became a farmer, he became territorial. He also fancied himself the owner of all within his territory. As "king of the castle" he effectively became a slave master, and the slaves he mastered were his "livestock," including his wife and children.

> But once a man has established himself as the head of a nuclear family occupying a base, he begins to regard it as a miniterritory. He feels…that however small and circumscribed the area, the female belonging to him should confine herself to it, and not wander onto the territory of other males. Once he becomes a tool maker and then begins accumulating property, he feels the property, like the female, should remain at the base; she

> becomes in his mind a part of the property. Whatever
> position he might occupy vis-à-vis other males, within
> his miniterritory he is the alpha, his dominance is
> absolute, and there is no one to exert it against except
> the female and her offspring. (Morgan 209)

The establishment of the division of labor and the nuclear family
during the age of the hunters and gatherers also produced territorial
feelings, but they became much stronger when the economy
became agricultural, according to Morgan. Farming demanded a
lot of work. The farmer needed the help of strong sons, sons his
mate could give him. She became a most valuable piece of
property (209-10). When a human is thought to be property, that
human is a slave. John Lennon minced no words when he sang,
"Woman is the Nigger of the World";

> Woman is the nigger of the world, yes she is
> If you don't believe me take a look at the one you're with
> Woman is the slaves [*sic*] of the slaves
> Yeah (think about it)
> --John Lennon

Woman as baby producer not only provided field hands,
she also gave to man a kind of tangible immortality—a part of him
could live on in his children. In addition, his children, particularly
his sons, could inherit all he had worked so hard for all his life. He
could pass on his knowledge of the world and his wealth. (Shlain,
271-304). Woman as mother, a maker of babies, was invaluable.

> The farmer took a wife, and the wife took a child or two
> or three—and the farmer prospered.
> Agriculture created so much wealth that now men in
> general could take more of their attention away from
> the problem of merely keeping alive and devote it to
> making life pleasurable. Woman, that most versatile of

> chattels, had her uses here also, as concubine and
> prostitute. (Morgan, 210-11).

Men have been accused of thinking that women are divided into two groups: virgins or whores. Another twofold division could be argued: that of workhorses or circus ponies—the former slaved and produced heirs, and about the latter—well, men do love a good ride!

So why didn't woman just cut and run? For one thing, she too had become territorial. She'd grown attached to her home: the pumpkin into which "Peter, Peter, Pumpkin Eater" had put her out of fear that he could not keep her. For another, by now the culture was such that she'd have no support for her flight. She no longer had close female friends that she could count on; her support system was divided up and living in their own respective "pumpkins." She was alone and trapped.

Wait! She wasn't alone; she had children by her side, on her lap, hiding in the folds of her skirt—that was the main reason why she allowed this to happen in the first place and why she now puts up with it. It's for the children. She realizes that a child is usually better off when raised with both a mother and a father.[3]

"Women, above all, want their children," states Morgan (214). The wife
takes the child, willingly, eagerly, and lovingly (in most cases). The man's basic need for sex and the woman's ache for a child insure the production of children (if lucky, she enjoys the sex too). Morgan hits the nail on the head when she says, "The children are really at the heart of it all" (212). Without children, there is no future. Without children, we become an extinct species. But is it necessary that the female half of our species be subordinate—that when the two become one, that "one" is the male? Is it necessary that a woman be cut off from her natural support system—other women, daughters, sisters, etc.? It is ironic that other women, who should be a woman's greatest support, are now too often considered contenders rather than allies—too many centuries of in-house training.

Conclusion

The development and spread of agriculture slowly but surely led to the enslavement of woman. Animals were domesticated, plants were domesticated, and woman allowed herself to be domesticated. An agrarian society is a patriarchal society, and the roots of patriarchy are deep and strong, extending into the industrial age and beyond. In a patriarchy, a woman has little power. She is like the "caged bird" about which Maya Angelou writes:

> The caged bird sings with a fearful trill
> Of things unknown but longed for still
> And [her] tune is heard on the distant hill
> For the caged bird sings of freedom.

Who Controls?

Woman, It's Your Call

"Who has forbidden women to engage in private and individual studies? Have they not a rational soul as men do?...I have this inclination to study and if it is evil I am not the one who formed me thus—I was born with it and with it I shall die."
Sor Juana Ines de la Cruz—Letter to Father Nunez 1681, Mexico.

"We deny the right of any portion of the species to decide for another portion what is and what is not their 'proper sphere.' The proper sphere for all human beings is the largest and highest they are able to attain to.
"Harriet Taylor Mill in 1850, England

"The myth that men are the economic providers and women, mainly, are mothers and care givers in the family has now been thoroughly refuted. This family pattern has never been the norm, except in a narrow middle-class segment."
Gro Harlem Brundtland, Prime Minister of Norway, 1995

Cultures that oppress women, deny them the leveling power of education, and keep them out of society and the workplace, are wasting a valuable resource. "Wilful [*sic*] waste brings woeful want," said Thomas Fuller (1654-1734). Men and women were meant to be complementary equals—their respective, unique talents working together for the good of all. It was so in the beginning.

Back in the time when we were all hunters and gatherers, women and men had their separate roles, but they lived and worked as equals ("Science of the Sexes"). The advent of agriculture led to the downfall of woman. Man became hung up on possessions—his property, his children, and his woman. Man, particularly when young, is the sex in "a state of full-blown 'estrus' *all the time*," according to Dr. Leonard Shlain (346). Man craved woman for sex, and so he made her into a sex object whose job it was to acquiesce to his sexual needs and to produce children, especially sons. Sons were important. They could learn from him, help him in the fields, and inherit his property when he died.

As a possession, woman was expected to stay at home and stay out of social, political, and economic affairs. These expectations were reinforced by man-controlled education and religion. People were indoctrinated as to what women were like. Men defined themselves, and then arrogantly defined women.

Times have changed.[4] Advances in health care have drastically cut the death rate of children and of mothers in childbirth. Effective birth control methods allow women to control the number of births, and mothers in developed countries are having fewer children. Fewer children means fewer years spent caring for children. Technology has lightened women's work immensely. Women now have time to contribute to civilization, but too often they hold back or settle for less than all they could be. This is understandable when you consider that both women and men are indoctrinated from birth with patriarchy's definition of woman. The time has come to show not only men, but also--and especially—women, that they are so much more. Woman, you better believe it, the world needs your talents. In fact the countries that will prosper and pull ahead of others are those that use to the fullest the unique talents of women.

Those in the "biology is destiny" camp say that the most important use of women's talents is producing and raising children. They are right about the greatness and importance of that role, though women receive little respect and appreciation for the huge amount of labor involved; in fact, women are often treated with contempt because of their reproduction systems: menstruation makes the woman "unclean" and many unnecessary hysterectomies have been done to get rid of that "troublesome uterus."

Who Controls?

If biology alone is woman's destiny, we are doomed to propagate ourselves into extinction. Lester Brown, population expert, predicts that by 2050 three billion people will join the six billion already here, for a total of nine billion people on an Earth that does not grow in size.

It is not so much actual *square footage* that is threatened; it is Earth's resources, resources that we need to live. A United Nations report warns: "More than half of humanity will be living with water shortages, depleted fisheries and polluted coastlines within fifty years because of a worldwide water crisis" (Vergano). Water shortages mean food shortages, leading to malnutrition and hunger. We are using too much of everything; "forests are shrinking, fisheries are collapsing…soils are eroding, [and] grasslands are deteriorating."

Lester Brown sees a global crisis coming. He wonders how world leaders will respond when the world's population hits nine billion by 2050, with falling water tables, rising temperatures, declining food production accompanied with rising food prices. Will it take all these critical problems to finally get our leaders to wake up? To force them to fundamentally rethink what we've been doing? And do we have enough time to save ourselves?

We need to start the rethinking process right now. Forewarned is forearmed. If we begin, right now, to stabilize or even decrease population growth, we can avert the crisis. This will require a major change in the world's patriarchal system, for it means controlling births, and this must be done by putting control of fertility into the hands of those who give birth. With the wide array of reliable contraceptives available today, contraceptives that prevent pregnancy by stopping the release of an egg, stopping ovulation, women can have as many or as few children as they want. If they choose to have only one or two children, they make their "biological destiny," into a part-time job at best. They will need other outlets for their energy.

Women in developed countries have found these outlets. They have reduced family size,[5] giving them time to complete educations and enter the workplace. Many choose not to have a family—ever, or not just yet. According to a June 2010 survey by the Census Bureau, forty-seven percent of American women between the ages of fifteen and forty-four have decided to delay or forgo motherhood.[6]

Women are not immune to ambition. They naturally want the power and influence that they deserve for hard work. Some women believe that the way to obtain coveted power and influence is to be as much like men as possible. They may try, but they won't succeed. Men and women are quite different. According to Helen Fisher, world-renowned anthropologist, the brain of each sex is built in certain ways, and then culture molds it. She firmly states, "You cannot make a girl into a boy or a boy into a girl" ("Science of the Sexes").

Our patriarchal world has long valued, even magnified, the talents of men, but has often not recognized; or worse yet, has denigrated the talents of women. The skewed view of women held by the Afghan husband of a brutally abused child bride is shared by many men, to some degree: "Women don't have the same brains like men. They are very forgetful. They can't make big decisions. You should ask your own Western doctors about this. It has been proven that women are not like men." (quoted in Raghavan)

He is correct when he says, "Women are not like men," and "Women don't have the same brains like men." He believes that the difference is in quality, and he justifies the subjugation of women. He is wrong. The difference is not in quality; it is in kind.[7]

For twenty years Fisher studied the bodies and minds of 750 people making up the Hadza of northern Tanzania. They neither garden nor raise animals. They are hunter/gatherers, such as our ancestors were around three million years ago.

The men hunt and gather wild honey. To this end, they have developed skills that make them successful hunters. Their eyes track movements; the faster the movement, the better they can track it.[8] They take risks as they aggressively go after big game. The spatial skills they evolved over time enable them to bring their kill home to the group. Today's men evidence these same strengths ("Science of the Sexes").

The women, the gatherers, are at the group's center. What they gather makes up 80 percent of the evening meal. Their peripheral vision is better than that of men's and this is useful in spotting edible plants and in keeping children in sight. As they work together, they talk to each other and to their children. The making of language evolved two million years ago, and the women used it as a tool to hold relationships together and to raise their children, as women do today. Fisher says, "Talking women survived" ("Science of the Sexes").

The unique skills acquired by each sex in prehistory account for many of the distinct differences that exist between the male and female brain today ("Science of the Sexes"). Magnetic Resonance Imaging (MRI) has revealed many differences. Michael Gurian, psychologist, says that 100 structural differences exist between the brain of a woman and the brain of a man ("Measures of Difference"). Laboratory experiments, observing reactions of boys and girls to arranged situations, prove this to be true. Before we go on and cite experiments done to prove the existence of these differences, a word of caution from Simon Baron-Cohen, writer and researcher: "Not all men have the male brain, and not all women have the female brain. In fact, some women have the male brain, and some men have the female brain." His book, *The Essential Difference: The Truth about the Male and Female Brain,* claims only that more men have the male brain, and more women have the female brain. He deals with statistical averages, and does not make assumptions.

Fisher, quoting Nyborg,[9] says essentially the same thing; all of us are an "intriguing amalgam of male and female shaped by biology":

> The fetal brain grows slowly and unevenly, so different parts of the hormones also change continuously … tides of powerful sex hormones can masculinize one part of the brain while they leave another region untouched. As

a result, every human being lies somewhere along a continuum that ranges from superfeminine to hypermasculine, depending on the amount and timing of hormones the individual was doused with in the womb. (quoted in Fisher, *First Sex,* xviii)

Experiments Show Brain Differences: The Hadza study showed women to be better at communication and men to be more aggressive. Michael Lewis, of the Institute of Child Development in New Jersey, set up some experiments that show this to be true. In an experiment involving 200 children, one-year-olds were put behind a barrier separating them from their mothers. When a boy was so separated, he attacked the barrier, trying to bring it down. A girl, faced with the same situation called for help. Lewis believes that hormones in the womb account for the difference in response: testosterone in the boy's case, and estrogen in the girl's ("Science of the Sexes").

In another experiment designed to measure language skills, fifty twelve-year-olds were told to write as many words as possible beginning with the letter "B." Boys and girls were given the same amount of time to do this. The girls averaged thirty-four words and the boys twenty-five. Girls tend to have better verbal memory, and to be more proficient in written prose, articulation, and in coming up with the right word ("Science of the Sexes"). If Fisher is right, and only talking women survived, this makes perfect sense.

Lewis used two-year-olds to test reactions to a doll whose arm comes off when it is being held. He wanted to know which sex was more sympathetic. A girl confronted with such a doll, tries to fix it. She feels responsible. A boy in the same situation does not feel responsible. It's not his fault. Girls were clearly more sympathetic ("Science of the Sexes").

In a test of empathy, the ability to "put yourself in someone else's shoes," an eight-year-old girl stood alone on a busy sidewalk for twenty minutes. Seventy-four people passed. Of that number, seven women stopped, but not one man did. Clearly, the women showed more empathy. Lewis suggests that females focus on themselves in order to better understand others. Another factor leading to the development of empathy is the oxytocin stimulated by childbirth. This hormone helps mothers nurture their offspring and gives them greater ability to empathize. Not only do the children benefit from this ability to empathize, but so do men, the sick, and women themselves ("Science of the Sexes").

Though men have trouble expressing most emotions, anger is the exception. Fisher says they do not hide that emotion. Neuroscientists Rueben and Racquel Gur wanted to find out which sex was better at *recognizing* emotion. They found in their research that women are better. They use less "brain space" to do so than do men. It's just easier for women ("Science of the Sexes").

Sebastian Kraemer, psychiatrist, tested girls and boys for "precise manipulation of objects." They stacked blocks. The girls proved to be better at it because they were more patient and more precise. In another test, girls and boys were told to draw a bicycle from memory. Here the boys excelled. Boys are more drawn to mechanical things; they want to know "how things work" ("Science of the Sexes").

According to Fisher, this is true of boys all over the world. When their brains "flood with testosterone" at puberty, they develop mechanical skills, become good at geometry, and the challenge to make or fix something turns them into engineers. Their more compartmentalized brain allows them to "zero in" on a project or problem on one thing at a time; they, according to Kraemer, have a "spotlight" mind ("Science of the Sexes").

If the human male's mind is a spotlight, the human female's mind is a floodlight. Psychiatrist Sebastian Kraemer says a woman's brain has a thicker connection, or "bridge," between the two sides of her brain. Estrogen is responsible for this superior connection; it enables her see the "big picture." It is easier for her to multitask and absorb information simultaneously. These abilities make her a natural businesswoman ("Science of the Sexes").

The "spotlight" and "floodlight" metaphors apply to sexual lives as well. The spotlight quality of the male mind, driven by his need for sex, his "sexual furnace [being] set at full blast *all the time"* (Shlain 109), was evident whenever Buck Owens sang, "Wham bam thank you ma'm I'll be on my way." The chorus of "A Little Less Talk and a Lot More Action" is even more explicit:

> A little less talk if you please
> A lot more loving is what I need
> Let's get on down to the main attraction
> With a little less talk and a lot more action.
> (lyrics by Scott Davis)

Songs also reveal the floodlight quality of woman's sexual needs. According to Fisher, a woman is aroused by romantic words and images; she fantasizes about affection and commitment; and she likes being touched all over her body. The country music group "Exile" zoomed to the top of the music charts in 1978 with the song, "I Want to Kiss You All Over." The Pointer Sisters knew what it was all about too, with their song, "Slow Hand":

> I want somebody who will spend some time
> Not come and go in a heated rush
> I want somebody who will understand
> When it comes to love, I want a slow hand.

With such diametrically opposed sexual needs as exemplified by these songs, is it any wonder that men and women have a hard time meeting, let alone understanding each other's desires when it comes to sex?

"Women have a robust libido," says Fisher, "different from that of men … just as durable across the life course" (*First Sex,* 204). Women, being longer-lived than men, can enjoy sex longer—provided they can find a partner. "Men," to quote Fisher, "are expendable. Though they can recover from heavy exercise faster than women--due to their greater lung capacity and greater number of red blood cells--they have trouble 'pacing themselves,' where women do not." Men die sooner; they also succumb to low libido. (This condition is now battled by millions of pills: Viagra,

Cialis, Levitra, etc.) The testosterone that made them manly is "not good for long-term health," says Kraemer ("Science of the Sexes").

Women shine when it comes to sheer endurance and stamina; their cells are more resilient. Grandmothers, believes Fisher, were needed to help young mothers raise children. Menopause, rendering a woman incapable of conception, made this possible. Menopause, in effect, causes estrogen levels to decrease and this "unmasks" testosterone. The unmasking of testosterone makes menopausal women more assertive, more outspoken ("Science of the Sexes"). These "grandmothers with attitude" did much to increase the survival rate of children.

In our patriarchal world, "woman's place" is in the home; whereas, men's place is all over the map. They're here and there and everywhere, showing women what they can do. They have defined themselves into positions of power and adventure. They have done much. One thing, however, they must no longer do, and that is to define women. Women need to do this for themselves. Their special talents are vitally needed in today's world. Men will not want to let them in. The biggest hurdle of all will be convincing women of their own worth after so many centuries of being put down, put upon, and put into their "place."

Conclusion

Men and women are not alike, but their differences are in kind, not quality. Their differences are meant to complement each other. Where men are aggressive and like to take risks, women are patient and cautious. Men have spatial skills that make them navigators and engineers. They have "spotlight' brains that can concentrate on mechanics, on fixing things, on finding out how things work.

Women possess the communication skills so necessary in today's world where speaking and writing clearly, finding just the right word, is crucial. Their ability to multitask and absorb information simultaneously makes them natural businesswomen. Women's "floodlight" brains can see the big picture.

It's true; women are more emotional. They can express and detect a wide range of emotions. Men, on the other hand, often hide their emotions, except for anger, and they have trouble recognizing emotions in others. Each style has its place.

When it comes to the physical, men, built for action, have trouble "pacing themselves"—this truth extends into their sex life. The testosterone that makes them manly, also gives them a shorter lifespan. Fisher believes women live longer because grandmothers were needed to help raise the children—it was a survival mechanism. Women still live longer, and when menopause decreases the estrogen and "unmasks" the testosterone within them, they become fearlessly able to speak their minds (*First Sex,* 182-7).

Mentally, emotionally, and physically, women are not the "weaker sex." They differ from men in many ways (and vice versa), but both are capable of great courage. Both women and men can love, hate, and seek revenge for wrongs. Both sexes are, above all, equal in humanity, being endowed with special talents that are meant to complement each other. Women, defining themselves, will change the world. Just how, we don't yet know, but Fisher, in her book *The First Sex,* has some definite ideas about what is to come.

The Future According to Fisher

Fisher, as an anthropologist, has been watching human progress for quite a long time, and she believes that women "will change the business and professional world." Women's skills are needed, and as they occupy positions of influence, they will use their skills to the advantage of all. Women will change what we see, hear, and read. She predicts less violence in media content and more stories with greater complexity and attention paid to human values. Women will be more "real" and so will human relationships in general, showing the age and ethnic diversities of real life. Both news and film will enlarge their range of topics covered, and we'll see more talk shows, more visual and performing arts, and more stories for children. In sum, we will have our perspectives widened on every issue and topic, both foreign and domestic *(First Sex,* 190-191).

As for women in particular, Fisher sees more American women earning advanced degrees than American men. Women, with their greater flexibility, imagination, patience, and empathy, will be stars in the teaching profession. As students are taught greater respect for ethnic, racial, and cultural diversity, and as more flexible gender roles are encouraged, the thinking of millions will be positively affected (191). Women will have a greater influence on the business world. Products and advertising will change. Clients, treated more personally, will take center stage. The workplace will become more flexible as work and family life become more balanced. In fact, many women will choose to work for themselves, creating their own flexible, tailor-made schedules. The service professions, already the domain of women, will grow in new and interesting ways. The law, whether it is to be made, interpreted, or enforced, will be more and more the province of women; they are the "great communicators." Female lawyers and judges "may bring about a broader, more contextual view of crime and justice in the courtroom." In fact, all laws dealing with women, children, and minorities will keenly interest them (191-192).

Women will change the healing professions, says Fisher. She sees group practices and wellness clinics flourishing. There will be greater efforts to determine causes of diseases rather than just treating the symptoms: a holistic approach. We will see the establishment of more support groups for the seriously ill and dying. Non-profit groups of all kinds will proliferate and with their money and "clout" will influence legislation, improving the lot of women, children, minorities, the elderly, the poor, and the disabled. "As women continue to shed the remnants of agrarian tradition and their second-class status, they will apply their many natural talents in the marketplace; subtly, at times dramatically, women will change the world" (192-3).

Veiled Thoughts

She thinks:

Who is this man I'm soon to wed?
To him, am I just someone to bed?
A brood mare—a mouse—
A slave in his house?
Will I be his companion—a true trusted friend,
Someone he'll cherish and love 'till the end?
A vale of tears or a life of bliss?
How did I get into this?

He thinks:

Beyond the veil I cannot see
If she's excited or wants to flee.
Hot sex on demand
When she's mine to command,
Will warm all our nights.
It's part of my rights!
Hot food on the table, she better be able
To cook and to clean—you know what I mean.

Montaigne compares marriage to a cage, "the birds outside despair to get in and those within despair to get out." Samuel Rogers writes, "It doesn't much signify whom one marries, for one is sure to find next morning that it was someone else." Here's a woman's take on marriage: O! how short a time does it take to put an end to a woman's liberty (Fanny Birney, *Diary*, 20 July 1768). Sammy Cahn's song, "The Tender Trap," sums up the ambivalence:

      And then you wonder how it all came about

Who Controls?

> It's too late now there's no getting out
> You fell in love, and love is the tender trap.

For men, love is a "tender trap" in the sense that they have "forsaken all others" and from now on will get their affection, tender loving, solely from their own wives—they are trapped, tenderly. (Shlain writes in *Sex, Time and Power*, that men never forgive women for making them "forsake all others" (348).)

Women also find marriage a tender trap, particularly if they have children. The love of a mother for her child is a tender trap. Most mothers will do almost anything necessary for the welfare of their children: turn a blind eye to infidelity, put up with a husband that's a drinker, and endure physical and emotional abuse. She's trapped by her tender love for her children.

Marriage is difficult, and adding to its difficulty are the differences between men and women, making misunderstanding a given. Professor Henry Higgins, in *My Fair Lady*, speaks for countless men when he laments the fact that a woman can't be "more like a man." The situation is particularly difficult for a woman, because when she marries, she becomes man's subordinate. This is not right. Marriage still has value, yet it is an institution in need of radical reform.

Marriage is good for children. Parents who love their children and each other make for a marriage in which children thrive, but too many marriages these days are not like that, and too many children are being raised in broken homes.

All over the industrialized world, the divorce rate is increasing. According to 2002 statistics, close to 46% of new marriages in America end in divorce. America is seventh on the list, with Sweden at the top with almost 55%; the country with the least divorce is India [10]

Divorce is not good for children, writes Leslie Foulkes-Jamison, Ph.D., they suffer multiple stressors; they know things will change for them after a divorce, but not knowing *how* things will change, is frightening to most. It may take a child two years or more to adjust to the divorce; in fact, some children can carry adjustment problems into adulthood. The age of the child at the time of divorce makes a difference. A preschooler will have trouble understanding what is going on, and they are emotionally needy. Frequently they blame themselves for the divorce Children between the ages of six and eight often fantasize about their parents getting together again.

Gender also makes a difference in a child's reaction to divorce. Girls tend to be more anxious and withdrawn; boys, on the other hand, often display aggressive and disobedient behavior. Frequently adding to the distress of the children and the custodial adult is a reduction in their standard of living (Foulkes-Jamison, Ph.D.).

Though many marriages end in divorce, some marriages actually seem to have been "made in heaven." The noted historians, Will and Ariel Durant, Pulitzer Prize winners, collaborated brilliantly during their long, successful writing careers and their marriage. Actors are notorious for their infidelities and many marriages, but two well-known couples, Jessica Tandy and Hume Cronyn and Joanne Woodward and Paul Newman, managed to stay together. In the cases mentioned, the couples combined their love of work with their love for each other. "Love does not consist in gazing at each other, but in looking together in the same direction" (Antoine de Saint-Exupéry). These couples were more than partners, they were true companions.

Such marriages are rare in our patriarchal world. Men feel the need to control women, especially their sexuality and their reproductive rights (Shlain, 349). This need to control tramples on women's human rights; it makes slaves of women. Control is usually accomplished through marriage, in spite of Article 16, items (1) and (2), of the United Nation's "Universal Declaration of Human Rights," which tries to insure that each participant in marriage will have equal rights:

> 1. Men and women of full age, without any limitation due to race, nationality or religion, have the right to marry and to found a family. They are entitled to equal

rights as to marriage, during marriage and at its
dissolution.
2. Marriage shall be entered into only with the free and
full consent of the intending spouses
.

Notice especially the sentence at the end of Item #1:"They
are entitled to equal rights as to marriage, during marriage, and at
its dissolution." In too many marriages, this is ignored; the desire
for control is too strong.

Controlling an equal is shameful slavery; therefore, men
must find ways to demote and demean women as a way of
rationalizing their treatment of women. Men around countless
water coolers gleefully share jokes about women--their ignorance,
their looks, their body parts, and their habits.

Men also frequently make jokes about marriage, which is
often referred to as "wedlock"; and a wife is called a "ball-and-
chain." While a man may say he regrets ever marrying, it really has
a lot of advantages for him: he gets a cook, a housekeeper, regular
sex, and a longer, healthier, wealthier life than a single man
(Serena Gordon).[11] Most importantly he can be a father with a
sort of visible immortality.

Martin Luther's theory about men and women and how
they should relate to each other parallels the expectations of the
traditional Christian marriage, and as such, further demeans
women and strives to keep them shackled to the home:

> Men have broad and large chests, and small narrow
> hips, and are more understanding than women, who
> have but small and narrow chests, and broad hips, to the
> end they should remain at home, sit still, keep house,
> and bear and bring up children (Martin Luther: *Table
> Talk*, 725).

How, pray tell, does a woman keep house and bear and
bring up children while sitting still?

Who Controls?

The traditional marriage, in which a woman promised to obey the man, clearly demoted her to the status of a slave. Though "obey" has been removed from many Western marriage ceremonies, marriage is still a contract binding two people, and the man is considered the more important of the two.

History shows that men will do almost anything to keep the little woman at home and obedient. The chastity belt, a cruel device entering Europe from the East at the time of the Crusades, controlled a woman's genitals by encasing her in a welded, metal corset with a metal bar passing between her legs. This bar had two narrow slits edged with sharp teeth for bodily evacuation. It must have been painful and extremely irritating. It was also unsanitary. A woman could not possibly keep herself clean while wearing such a contraption (Rosalind Miles, 113-14).

For a thousand years, Chinese women's feet were mutilated by being tightly bound in childhood. A woman with tiny, bound feet could not walk very far without pain. In this country, as in so many others, where chastity was invaluable, her bound feet kept her within bounds. She could not be unfaithful— she could hardly walk! She was effectively controlled. A popular old adage states that a mother couldn't love her daughter and her daughter's feet at the same time. A daughter with unbound feet was not considered sexy or beautiful in that society. On the other hand, women with bound feet were considered "virtuous, beautiful, and sexy." Bound feet were the "ultimate marker of civility, according to Neo Confucian thinking. If the girl hoped to someday make a "good" marriage, she bound her feet (Vento).

Bad as chastity belts and bound feet sounds, clitoridectomy, or as some euphemistically refer to it, "genital circumcision," is worse, and it's happening right now. In some Mediterranean and Islamic countries, the clitoridectomy is an aspect of family honor. It sometimes involves the amputation of all external female organs, not just the clitoris, and it is mutilation. On occasion this mutilation results in death. The sole purpose of such genital mutilation is to take away from a woman the ability to enjoy sex, supposedly making them less apt to be unfaithful. An ironic twist: Pfizer, Inc., after eight years of testing 3,000 women, gave up on trying to prove that Viagra works on them. It doesn't work because the brain is a woman's crucial sex organ.

Why would any mother allow her daughter to be so mutilated? The answer is the same as the one given in Vento's writing about Chinese foot binding, the only change being that of body parts: a mother couldn't love her daughter and her daughter's …[clitoris] … at the same time; not if she wanted her daughter to make a "good" marriage; so, off with the clitoris!

In some Mediterranean and African countries where female chastity is a critical matter of virtue, public evidence of a bride's lost virginity is an important sequel to the marriage ceremony. A blood-stained sheet is hung outdoors the morning after the wedding night for all to see. A woman who is unable to demonstrate that she has lost her virginity to her new husband may be subject to violence, or even death (Sardone).

A priest in Brazil demands a certificate of virginity from a woman before he'll perform a marriage. Though residents of the small town in which he lives are angry with him, the priest stands firm, believing the church does not allow the marriage of non-virgins ("Priest Demands").

Women murdered for not being virgins, for not saving themselves for marriage, is a crime that has recently come to light in Europe where the number of so-called "honor killings" is rising. Many of these murders are thought to be the result of women involved in relationships that their families feel will bring them dishonor. In England and Wales, police are taking a second look at 100 murders they suspect might have been "honor" killings. Metropolitan police in London are reinvestigating old murder files that go back ten years. In some of the cases, the police suspect that the families hired contract killers to murder the women ("Europe Tackles").

Fueled with testosterone, the aggressive hormone, many men take matters into their own hands, as it were, and use brute force. A 1994 report from the U.S. Department of Justice has this to say: More than two-thirds of female victims of violent abuse knew their attacker. Boyfriends or husbands accounted for approximately 28%, acquaintances 35%, 5% were relatives, and the remaining 31% were strangers. The Report goes on to compare numbers of incidents of violence suffered by males and females, on average each year, and committed by an intimate. Females come out looking like in-house punching bags, experiencing ten times the amount of violent victimizations ("Commonly Used Domestic Violence Citations").

Conclusion

Enough statistics and examples: a picture of an institution in trouble emerges. Though marriage can be a loving union, too often it is a cruel trap; in fact, it can even be a death trap for women, and also a few men. This is unacceptable. Marriage must be made user-friendly for all concerned.

Men and women were meant to complement each other and to be companions. Only in a marriage of equals can this happen. Marriage is good for children; let's make it good for women and men, equally.

The User-Friendly Marriage

More things belong to marriage
than four bare legs in a bed.
--John Heywood

In most cases, a man and woman marry not only to experience "four bare legs in a bed," but also to have a family and to raise children that they hope will make them proud. The way traditional marriage is set up, this goal is becoming harder and harder to achieve. Our world seems to be shrinking. The quantity of information is so vast, and can now be disseminated so rapidly, that virtually all cultures are affected. Bob Dylan was correct when he wrote and sang, "The Times They Are A-Changin.'"

In the developed countries, divorce rates are on the rise, approaching or exceeding 50 percent, and it's harder raise children in a broken home. In countries where divorce rates are much lower, homes can still be broken, in an emotional sense. Women are frequently abused, and made to feel inferior. Unless we want to doom our children to repeat our mistakes, we need to install an upgrade to traditional marriage. Marriage must be made user-friendly.

Many believe that it's the divorce laws that need reforming. They make a good case for their point of view. Since the passage of the "no-fault" divorce laws in America, divorce rates have doubled. Broken families leave everyone poorer, especially women and children. According to experts, children of divorce are "twice as likely to be abused and become criminals and teen moms--even if they have stepparents." It was also found that "divorce doesn't end fighting in front of children--in most cases, it escalates it!" (quoted in "Americans for Divorce Reform"). Reforming divorce laws, however, is "putting the cart before the horse"; what we really need to do is reform the marriage laws, taking more account of human nature. In so doing, many of the reasons for divorce could be eliminated.

A first step for any country seeking to reform marriage, would be a hard look at the tenants outlined in the "Universal Declaration of Human Rights," Articles 7, 16, and 17:

Article 7

All are equal before the law and are entitled without any discrimination to equal protection of the law. All are entitled to equal protection against any discrimination in violation of the Declaration and against any incitement to such discrimination.

Article 16

1. Men and women of full age, without any limitation due to race, nationality or religion, have the right to marry and found a family. They are entitled to equal rights as to marriage, during marriage and at its dissolution

2. Marriage shall be entered into only with the free and full consent of the intending spouses.

3. The family is the natural and fundamental group unit of society and is entitled to protection by society and the State.

Article 17

1. Everyone has the right to own property alone as well as in association with others.
2. No one shall be arbitrarily deprived of [his or her] property.

"The Universal Declaration was adopted by the General Assembly on 10 December 1948 by a vote of 48 in favour, 0 against, with eight abstentions: the USSR, Ukrainian SSR, Byelorussian SSR, Yugoslavia, Poland, South Africa, Czechoslovakia, and Saudi Arabia." To their credit, countries are looking at these Articles. Countries such as Lebanon, Morocco, and China are reforming their marriage laws—some have already done so, others are in the planning stage.

No marriage reform is planned in the Scandinavian countries. Indeed, divorce and marriage seem destined to become non-issues. Increasingly, in Sweden, Norway, and Denmark, women are having babies outside of marriage and then not necessarily ever marrying. Having a baby without being married carries no stigma in Scandinavia (Noelle Knox).

Twenty-five-year-old Anne Marie Hansen's view on marriage is not unique. A man is chosen because he would be a good father; then a different man is chosen to be a husband. Anne Marie Hansen says that her friends who are mothers, have decided that the children are their own (N. Knox).

There is no real pressure from religion to marry. State churches exist in the Scandinavian countries, but few people attend. When asked directly why they choose not to marry, many answer that it is too great a commitment (N. Knox).

Many Americans may agree with Scandinavians on the commitment part, but religion still plays a strong role in America, serving to overcome commitment fears. In addition, births outside of marriage are as yet frowned upon, though they have tripled! Americans still value the sentiments expressed in the song, "Love and Marriage," especially the last verse (lyrics by Sammy Cahn):

> Love and marriage, love and marriage,
> Go together like a horse and carriage.
> Dad was told by mother,
> You can't have one without the other.

Yes, we value these sentiments, but ever more frequently, don't act on them. Because of the American stigma against "out-of-wedlock" births, many couples march to the altar if the woman is pregnant, only to march into divorce court later.

In fact, America has one of the highest divorce rates in the world. We may value marriage, but we don't value it enough if we marry with the thought that if it doesn't work out, we can easily get a divorce. This is wrong. We are shortchanging our children and ourselves. At least the Scandinavians realize that marriage takes commitment, and because they take this commitment so seriously, they seldom marry. They are honest. As things stand now, Americans have a window of opportunity in which marriage reform is possible, provided it is thought worth the effort.

Is marriage worth preserving? Noelle Knox says that in spite of Scandinavians "turning away from marriage," their quality of life has not suffered. In the United Nations 2004 quality-of-life survey, Norway ranked first and Sweden second; in fact, both countries have kept this ranking since 1995. The United States came in eighth. Keep in mind that this survey concerned a lot more than marriage; it included information about income and education levels, health care and longevity.

What works in the Scandinavian countries may not work well for other countries, including America. Take, for example, the practice of cohabitation. In Sweden it is more common to live together and have children, than it is to marry and have children (Knox). It is true that cohabitation is becoming more common in America, and children are often born to such couples. In fact, between the years 1980 and 1990, the number of children born to cohabiting couples doubled: "One child in eight was born to a cohabiting, unmarried couple. Forty percent of all children will spend some time with a cohabiting couple" (quoted in "Study: Marriage Produces"). As we might expect, children are affected by these changes. Just how they are affected must be determined in order to answer intelligently the question of whether or not marriage is worth saving.

Sociologists Manning and Smock, studied 6,500 children born to mothers less than thirty years old. Of this number, one thousand children were born to cohabiting, never married couples, and 5,500 children were born to parents in first marriages. "By the child's first birthday, 15 percent of the cohabiting parents split and 4 percent of the married couples divorced. By the time the child reached age 5, half of the unmarried parents broke up, while only

15 percent of the married couples separated" (quoted in "Study: Marriage Produces").

When a couple separates or divorces, the mother usually gets custody of the children, especially minor children. A Hudson Institute study found that "nearly four out of every 10 children are being raised without fathers" (quoted in "Children Need Fathers"). More results of growing up without a father:

> (1) Among long-term prison inmates, 70 percent grew up without fathers, as did 60 percent of rapists and 75 percent of adolescents charged with murder
> (2).Fatherless children are three times more likely to fail school, require psychiatric treatment and commit suicide as adolescents.
> (3) They are also up to 40 times more likely to experience child abuse compared with children growing up in two-parent families. ("Children Need Fathers")

Researchers Dougherty and Kurosaka, found that "motherless homes are 56 percent more likely to result in teen pregnancy among girls." The study did not find any significant relationship between motherless homes and male adolescent delinquency.

Children from stable families do better in school, are less apt to have early adolescent sex, and are less apt to be delinquent ("Study: Marriage Produces"). In addition, healthy marriages make for healthier kids. In a 1988 health and well-being survey, Dawson compared the health of children from disrupted homes with that of children living with both biological parents. Selected findings show the following: a 20 to 35% greater risk of injury for children from disrupted marriages; a 50% greater risk of developing asthma; increased risk of speech defects in children living with never-married mothers; more professional help needed for children having emotional or behavioral problems—significantly higher for those children living with formerly married mothers (Dawson quoted in Stanton).

Who Controls?

"Married with Children" is the best way to go. This being the case, marriage--for couples who want to be parents--needs to become a stronger, better institution. You may have heard this joke: "Marriage is an institution, and who wants to live in an institution?" Answer: children do. It's good for them. We need to make marriage good for parents too. We can make marriage more user-friendly by paying more attention to human nature.

We've all heard the saying, "Marry in haste; repent at leisure." Another old saying gives us the reason: "Love is blind." Researchers at University College London discovered that falling in love could actually affect the circuitry in the brain to such an extent that critical social assessment of others is suppressed; in other words, one can become blind to another's faults. Professor Leng of the University of Edinburgh, doing research in this area, hopes it will lead to new treatments for people with relationship problems ("Love's Strange Effect").

In the meantime, to quote another old saying, "Forewarned is forearmed." If we are aware that this giddy feeling may not be true love, that it may just be lust or infatuation, we can bide our time, knowing "Time will tell." If it's only lust or infatuation, the feeling will fade in approximately three years (Fisher, "Biology"). The song, "You've Lost That Loving Feeling," describes the end of what was NOT true love. To paraphrase the song: a man notices that no longer does his love close her eyes when they kiss. When she touches him, her touch no longer feels tender. She tries to hide her loss of feeling for him, but he knows that she's "lost that loving feeling."

> Now it's gone, gone, gone
> Whoa-oh...[12]

The wise couple will not finalize anything until those three years are up, and then if they still have that loving feeling, if they care deeply for each other, they are ready for commitment. Patience in a relationship will do much to decrease the divorce rate. Divorce commonly occurs early in marriage, and then it declines (Fisher, "Biology"). Putting off marriage for three or four years would get couples through those dangerous divorce-prone years.

Many couples are waiting. In fact, younger women aged twenty to twenty-four are putting off marriage. In 1970, 36 percent in that age bracket had never married, but by 2003 the number that had never married in that age group, had risen to 75 percent. Among men in the same age bracket, 55 percent had never married in 1970, but by 2003 the number that had never married in the twenty to twenty-four age group, had risen to 86 percent (Armas, "Men, Women in No Hurry").

Society has become more accepting of cohabiting couples. That may be one reason for the rising first-time marriage age for men and women. Jean Landers, a thirty-year-old law student, thinks living together is a requirement before marriage. She believes it's the way to find out if you are compatible (Armas).

People considering long-term relationships are becoming more cautious; they don't want to make a mistake. This is particularly true for a woman who wants a family, as she needs "extensive male parental investment. Fathers everywhere help feed, teach, support, and defend their children." Not only do the father's genes matter, but his resources do as well. In fact, even if the woman has a good income and earned status, she still prefers a mate with good financial prospects, as was true in the past (Wright).

Women need to study a prospective mate, and to beware of men who exaggerate their level of commitment. One study, mentioned by Wright, found that, unlike females, males are much more apt to describe themselves as "more kind, sincere, and trustworthy" than they really are. Women, remember the old adage: "Actions speak louder than words."

About male selectivity, Wright goes on to say, "Men will have sex with just about anything that moves, given an easy chance," but they become more discriminating when looking for a long-term mate. For the short-term, men will choose a woman who appears "easy" or promiscuous, but for a long-term relationship, he prefers a less attractive female, meaning one who looks less sexually experienced. Men also prefer younger women because they are more fertile (Wright)[13]. Men want to pass on their genes.

If we agree that divorce is harmful to children, and that the best place to raise children is within stable marriages, then marriage is definitely worth saving. Only people ready for a serious commitment should marry. Couples "falling in love" are only "novitiates"; they need time to discover if this "love" is true. It may be lust or infatuation, which means that, they will lose "that loving feeling."

The following is a plan for marriage reform that works with human nature rather than against it. Prospective spouses would register as a couple, and obtain their "learner's permit." They would be encouraged not to have children; this includes the adoption of children. This should not be a problem for heterosexual couples in these days of various, and reliable, birth control. After a minimum three years, if they feel their love is "rock solid" and lasting, or as Ira Gershwin put it—

> In time the Rockies may crumble
> Gibraltar may tumble
> They're only made of clay
> Oh, our love is here to stay.

Then they would take "final vows," at a civil or a religious ceremony, and get a marriage license. The marriage license entitles them to any privileges the state grants to married people, and it also entitles them to start a family if they so desire.

The idea of "covenant marriage," which is preceded by counseling, is slowly catching on. It certainly is in keeping with our ideals. We believe each individual is entitled to "life, liberty, and the pursuit of happiness." A couple chooses covenant marriage because they want a life together in which they are at liberty to choose what, to them, would produce the most stable marriage with the happiness we all pursue.

Covenant marriage is more protective of the huge amounts of personal investment called for by marriage. Income, lost professional opportunities (usually by the wife), old habits and amusements that need dropping or revision, and great amounts of sheer energy: all these go into a successful family. Such a commitment of resources needs protection so that a couple has peace of mind. Not only does covenant marriage lead to more peace of mind; it also provides a hedge against temptation; it helps to secure the couple's future. It is the civilized thing to do (Olson). It's also the child-friendly thing to do.

Though Louisiana was the first state to make covenant marriage legal (1997), Arkansas and Arizona soon followed. People who are already married in these states, have the choice of changing marriage to a covenant marriage. Other states are considering the creation of legal covenant marriages. These states include California, Florida, Georgia, Indiana, Iowa, Kansas, Maryland, Minnesota, Mississippi, Missouri, Nebraska, New Mexico, Oklahoma, Oregon, South Carolina, Tennessee, Texas, Utah, Virginia, Washington, and West Virginia (Wikipedia). Before all covenant marriage, new or "conversion," counseling is required.

Though supposedly the "land of the free and the home of the brave," there are those who oppose the idea of giving partners the choice of a covenant marriage, thinking that this exercise of their mutual will could result in the erosion of "prescriptive authority." They fear the "privatization" of marriage, conjuring up horrible scenarios of what the future may hold. They need to quit worrying and have the patience to wait for results from the states that have already embraced the idea.

Our user-friendly marriage upgrade, starts with a "practice," non-binding, childless "pre-marriage," lasting for about three years. At the end of the three years, the couple may either split or become united in a civil union, a "covenant marriage," or a traditional marriage that allows them to have children. Whatever type of marriage contract they enter into, it should guarantee as far as humanly possible, that if the family unit includes a child or children, the partners must stay together until the child or children are of legal age.

Who Controls?

A user-friendly marriage would include an "escape clause."
Though people intend that their marriage or civil union is for life,
it would be wise to include an "escape clause" that would let the
marriage dissolve after children reached adulthood if both partners
agree. The couple would take a long, critical look at their
partnership and at how each felt about its continuance. Consider
these lyrics by Ray Stevens from "Isn't It Lonely Together":

> Baby I think it's all in vain.
> We're just not birds of a feather.
> Isn't it lonely together?

If these lyrics describe how they now feel, they would go
their separate ways, as provided by this clause. On the other hand,
they could renew their promises to with each other if they felt like
Robert Browning when he wrote, "Grow old along with me! The
best is yet to be …"

This "escape clause" after children are grown is important
because people are living so much longer. Fifty or sixty, or
seventy, years together may seem hopelessly long to some couples
that have found they are not now even close to the "soul mates"
they thought they were. But if they knew that in twenty or thirty
years, they would have the freedom of another choice, they would
take heart and make the best of things. Remember, it's the children
that matter the most. On the other hand, those couples whose love
has endured and even grown stronger could happily reaffirm their
love as some couples now do, with a repeat performance of their
vows to each other. It's a win-win proposition, with the children
being the biggest winners.

Conclusion

America's no-fault divorce has made her the country with
one of the world's highest divorce rates. This is detrimental to her
most precious asset: children. Children do better if raised by their
biological parents in a stable marriage. Our divorce rate tells us
that it's time for a marriage overhaul.

Who Controls?

The "Universal Declaration of Human Rights" can serve as a guide, a starting point, to marriage reform. Several countries have reformed, or are in the process of reforming, their marriage laws. Other countries, such as those in Scandinavia, seem to have almost abandoned marriage. Yet most Americans believe that marriage is worth saving; it just needs to be made user-friendly.

The first step, a "pre-marriage" contract would give couples time to make sure they suited each other and that what they feel is "true love." If they believe that it's true love, they can take the second step and make their relationship more stable, through a civil union, a traditional marriage, or a covenant marriage. If their union includes a child or children, this second step would be in effect until any or all children became adults. At that time the third step kicks in, and they could decide whether to go their separate ways or continue on as a loving couple. This three-step marriage would be a win-win situation. Children would be raised in a secure home with their biological parents, the parents would have their huge investment in their marriage protected, and if things were not as rosy as they'd hoped in the long haul, they would have an avenue of escape once their children were grown.

Yes, "More things belong to marriage then four bare legs in a bed." The four bare legs often produce the patter of little feet, and they make marriage worthwhile and worth saving.

Birth Control: A Woman's Choice

She knelt in the dimly lit confessional and heard the priest explain to her why she could not use any birth control other than the Rhythm Method, and did she ever consider that it might be her thirteenth child who would support her, care for her, in her old age?

Despair filled her mind and her stomach clenched—thirteen children! She'd had five single births in seven years; now he was saying that she had eight more to go.

She stumbled out of the confessional and sank down onto the kneeler, her elbows on the backrest of the pew in front, hands cradling her head as tears seeped out of the corners of her eyes and thoughts collided. *Did he give me any penance? I don't know; I couldn't hear anything after the "thirteenth child" bit. Doomed, that's what I am. I'll go crazy before I reached that number of children, or else die, a bitter and angry old woman. It's not fair! I thought back to my grandmother who had delivered thirteen children, yes, thirteen!--just as he said, and then her husband, my grandfather, died of some kind of flu. It wasn't that she didn't want children; a farm wife was expected to produce farm hands, but she didn't want that many! She died of pneumonia in her sixties, angry, embittered, and alone--she and her daughters did not get along, and her sons were busy with farming. I did not want to end up like her.*

The Rhythm Method? I've had far more intimate moments with my thermometer than with my husband, and in spite of strictly observing the so-called "safe" days, I kept getting pregnant. The Rhythm Method did not work. I understood why it's referred to as "Vatican Roulette."

A woman provides a developing baby not only a home in her womb, but also the necessary nutrients needed for growth. Women have a fundamental, human right to be in control of reproduction. Unfortunately, religion, government, and culture, often disagree. In fact, some argue that a woman can choose to avoid pregnancy by avoiding sex, but having sex does not necessarily mean that a woman wants to get pregnant. The desire for sex is a strong, natural urge that should not be repressed, and it has other functions besides reproduction: it benefits mental and physical health, strengthens marriage bonds, and pleasures the participants.

Religion and reproduction: The **Eastern Orthodox Church,** "viewed marriage and sexual relations primarily as a means for procreation of children even to the point that intercourse within the marital state was tinged with sin if procreation was not the purpose" (George J. Jennings).[14]The encyclical, *Casti Connubi*, written in 1930, stated that abstinence was the only legal method of avoiding pregnancy The **Roman Catholic Church**, has outspokenly opposed birth control dating back to the time of Augustine. Pope Paul VI's view came out in his encyclical, *Humanae Vitae* in 1968, and it's the view in force today. Artificial contraception is "intrinsically evil," but natural family planning methods—abstinence during a woman's fertile time of the month, for example—are sometimes permissible. The Church fears that use of artificial means of birth control would lead to marital infidelity and to a loosening of moral standards in young people. Pope Paul VI also feared that men would "forget the reverence due a woman [and] reduce her to being a mere instrument for satisfaction of his own desires...." Stephen D. Mumford argues that the main reason behind the Church's continued opposition to artificial birth control is fear of losing papal authority if the dogma of infallibility should be contradicted ("Roman Catholicism").

Before the 1900's, all orthodox **Protestant** theologians opposed birth control. The sin of Onanism, *coitus interruptus*, was the main reason for their objection.[15] Thirty years later only Old Colony Mennonites, the Amish, officially opposed the practice of birth control (Brian Kopp, Ph.D.).

56

Mormonism, The Church of Latter Day Saints (LDS), issued an official public statement in 1969, discouraging birth control. It is "contrary to the teachings of the Church [to] artificially curtail or prevent the birth of children." A later Church handbook for local leaders discourages them from judging the private intimate relationships of their member ("Mormonism").

Islam places few restrictions on the use of contraceptives, with the exception of Turkey, where contraception is forbidden (Jennings). In Islamic countries that allow contraceptive use, surgical sterilization is not acceptable unless medically necessary. A Muslim considers it a form of castration. Also forbidden is the withdrawal method (*coitus interruptus*), unless the woman agrees to it ("Islamic Family Planning").

The **Jewish** religion's Torah says that a Jewish married couple should have at least one son and one daughter. Jewish men should not waste or destroy their "seed," sperm; therefore barrier contraceptive methods, vasectomies, and the withdrawal method are discouraged. A condom is permissible if its purpose is to avoid sexually transmitted diseases (STD's). Hormonal means of birth control, such as the birth control pill, is acceptable under certain conditions. Non-orthodox Jews commonly use whatever birth control they prefer, regardless of "waste of seed" ("Family Planning in the Jewish Religion").

Government and reproduction: Fear of too many people for a country's resources or of an increasing high rate of poverty, has in the past caused a government to limit the birth rate, usually by mandate. **China's** one-child policy, introduced in 1978, comes to mind. People having more than one child were punished by fines. The policy is controversial both inside and outside of China because of possible negative economic and social consequences.

In **India,** those with more than two children are not able to take part in local government. **Iran** has sharply reduced its birth rate by requiring males and females to take a mandatory contraceptive course before they can get a marriage license. The government emphasizes the benefits of smaller families ("Human Population Control").

Singapore has a roller-coaster, government-mandated, birth control history. First was the government's effort to reverse the boom in births that resulted after World War II. A "Stop at Two" program encouraged two-child families and also sterilization. The government put in place disincentives, penalizing parents for not stopping at two. It worked so well that after the 1980's, the government encouraged parents to have more children, as the birth rate had fallen below the replacement level. In 1987, the government put in place the "Have Three or More (if you can afford it)," and government strove to better the quality and the quantity of the population by discouraging low-income families from having children and promoting marriage between educated people ("Population Control in Singapore").

The Title X Family Planning program in the **United States** was enacted in 1970. It provides information, supplies, and access to contraception services. Title X funded clinics to help young individuals and low-income families decide on the right time to have children if they want to be parents. Title X's funding decreased drastically in 2006, and now Medicaid, with greatly increased funding, contributes to public family planning (Title X Family Planning).

A government finds its strength in people.[16] Numbers count. We learned this as little kids on the playground and as older kids in cliques, clubs, and gangs in school. *"Are you with us or against us? You have to choose."* We all wanted more members; it meant more strength, more clout. As long as we cannot control another gang's or our neighbor's behavior, we will try to make our group have as many or more members than a competing group, a potential enemy

Governments planning war seek to increase their population, and then after the war, they want to replace those lost, revitalize the country, with more births. Singapore was an example of the "encourage" followed by "discourage" of population growth. The Soviet Union, on July 8, 1944, established the honorary title "Mother Heroine." The title, along with a certificate bestowed by a Soviet governmental institution, and a medal were awarded to mothers bearing and raising ten or more children ("Mother Heroine"). The award was understandable in light of the fact that the Soviet Union lost around twenty-seven million people in World War II.

Religions are like any other group; they are in competition with other faiths for members. In India, Hindu revivalists are concerned about the substantial increase in the Muslim percentage of the Indian population. Muslims will not soon become a majority in the whole of India, but they will soon become a majority in strategic parts of the country, creating many "Kashmirs," if you will (Koanraad Elst).

With government urging women to produce soldiers for war, and religion urging women to produce members for the Church, how will women ever be able to claim their birthright, control of their own wombs? And we haven't even considered the effect of culture, closely intertwined with religion; a fact we must take into account in any discussion about birth control.

Culture and reproduction: "Culture," as defined by anthropologist, George J. Jennings, is the "total way of life or the design for living characterizing each human society." Sex and reproduction are tied to a culture's value system. For example, some cultures allow marriage of first cousins; others don't. In one culture there is guilt and shame associated with sex and reproduction, while in another, people feel free to discuss these subjects. Culture matters greatly when deciding how best to educate people about birth control.

Hebrew culture stresses the importance of children, especially in the Old Testament days when producing many children meant divine approval and blessing. Offspring had to carry on the family name; if not, the social structure was in danger (Jennings). The Torah has been interpreted to say that each Jewish family should have at least one son and one daughter (Rabbi Simmons).

Early Christians were split in their thinking about sex and reproduction. Some were on the side of celibacy, considering it to be superior to marriage and the raising of children. Roman Catholics made marriage a sacrament, with the intention of sanctifying the production of children. Nowadays, marriage is increasingly valued for companionship even when there is no thought of procreation (Jennings).

Hindu and **Buddhist** cultures apply few restrictions to birth control, either religious or legal. In India and China, contraception is legal and sterilization usually allowed (Jennings).

Middle Eastern countries have a population growth rate of almost three percent a year. This rate is exceeded only by some Latin American countries. Children are desired for their labor and for the prestige a large number of children give to the parents. But, as I mentioned before, contraception is allowed in most Islamic countries, with the exception of Turkey (Jennings).

In addition to strong religious influence, the **Latin American** culture affects the area's fertility, which is just under three percent. Though most may say they'd like smaller families, a husband's desire to prove his virility by having a child is present as soon as a couple marries—becoming a father proclaims his adulthood. With each child, he is advertising to the world his masculinity. The old double standard is alive and well in Latin America. The husband is expected to stray, the wife must not. She's been prepared for this role by her mother, who described sex as "ugly and unladylike." She does her conjugal duty because she believes, as does her husband, that "children reinforce the marital bond and reduce…unfaithfulness" (Jennings).

Male authority also contributes to the high birth rate in Latin America. Contraceptives interfere with a man's male authority, the authority that gives them the right to determine "the time, form, and frequency of coitus." Both men and women believe that birth control is injurious to health. Puerto Rican husbands and wives think contraceptive measures can cause cancer in women. As for the diaphragm, they fear that it can get trapped in the vagina and require surgical removal. Another myth: sterilization causes chronic illness and helplessness in women. Use a Condom? Men fear that it could get trapped inside the woman and kill her; besides that, condoms destroy the pleasure of intercourse. Couples tend to have an exaggerated sense of modesty; they hesitate to seek information about birth control. Jennings says that some of these distorted ideas are spread by religious zealots (Jennings).

All the above factors work against what is woman's fundamental right: the control of reproduction. She came with the equipment; she needs to be free to operate it as she sees fit. She will do the right thing for her and for Planet Earth. Robert Engleman, Vice President of the Worldwatch Institute, interviewed women in Africa, Asia, and Latin America over a period of twenty-five years. He wrote a book, *More Choice for Women Means More Sustainability*, about his findings:

> In countries that make personal control of reproduction possible, women invariably have two children or fewer on average.

> The answer to what women want, is not more children, but more for their children.

> Expanding the capacity of all women to choose when to bear children is …the surest route to achieving an environmentally sustainable population.

Societies that make it easy for women and their partners to plan their families, will enjoy gradually decreasing populations, reducing the challenge of building environmentally friendly, sustainable societies. According to Worldwatch President, Christopher Flavin (quoted in Engleman's book), "Population growth is a driving force behind some of today's most serious problems, including climate change and rising food prices."

Engleman has identified an approach to family planning that results in a gradual reduction in population, leading to sustainable societies with opportunity for all.

Women can and will help the Planet reach sustainability if they have easy access to truthful education about their bodies and their choices, counseling to help them make the right individual choice, with free birth control supplies if that is the choice.

Margaret Sanger was America's pioneer in reproductive health for women. She devoted fifty years of her life to improving the reproductive lives of women, and in 1965, a year after her death, the United States Supreme Court struck down the one remaining law prohibiting the private use of contraceptives.

Sanger saw what constant child-bearing did to a woman's health as she nursed her mother, dying of tuberculosis at the age of forty-nine. She blamed her mother's early death on her eighteen pregnancies—Sanger was number six of the eleven who lived. She wanted to help, so she became a nurse and later, in 1910, a home nurse and midwife on the Lower East Side of New York. The "sickness, misery, helplessness, and death that came to the poverty-stricken young mothers whose 'weary misshapen bodies' were destined to be thrown on the scrap heap before they were thirty-five!" undoubtedly reminded her of the cruel fate of her own mother .

In those days even doctors could not give out birth control information. This, Sanger could not accept. In 1914 she traveled to Europe to learn about contraceptive technology. She returned home and in 1916 Sanger opened the first United States birth control clinic in Brooklyn, New York. With her sister and a friend as her helpers, the clinic gave out birth control advice and sold contraceptives. In ten days they had counseled 500 women, and that was the end for the clinic, as the police then shut them down and jailed Sanger. She did gain a small victory, as the Court's judgment at her trial was worded in such a way that it allowed doctors to provide birth control information under the pretense of preventing venereal disease.

Who Controls?

In 1921, Sanger organized the American Birth Control League. It later became the Planned Parenthood Federation of American. She then campaigned for a female-controlled contraceptive, and her efforts led to the development of the first birth control pill in 1960. She was an American Hero.[17]

Because of thinkers and doers like Margaret Sanger women no longer need be cursed by the organ that should be a blessing: the womb. Enough of the manipulation by "the big three": religion, government, and culture. This "turn on the baby machine" then "turn off the baby machine" when things start to get a bit crowded must stop. Whose "baby machine" is it, anyway? Hers, of course, and decisions concerning reproduction and family planning also belong to her. So many choices for controlling the "whether, when, and how many" exist today, that it's not easy to decide.

Yet, decide we must in light of some very sobering statistics reported by Michael Ross, Ph. D., in Psychology Today (02 January 2012). Nearly one-half the pregnancies in America are unintended, with the highest number of unintended pregnancies among adolescents,[18] poor women, and African American women. In addition to being medically costly (increased risk of infant mortality and low birth rate babies), our society also pays dearly, in the form of welfare dependency and sometimes even child abuse and neglect.

Some more sobering facts: genital herpes affects forty-five million people in America—a million new cases every year. Sexually transmitted disease (STD's) rates are the highest in the developed world. Among some adolescent populations, chlamydia and gonorrhea have hit epidemic rates. We need to screen for disease and treat it, and also educate our young people on how to use condoms to prevent transmission of STD's (Ross).

Abstinence will not be considered as a method of birth control here, because it's the province of religion and personal moral ethics; besides, it doesn't work as a policy. In April of 2008, a congressional committee examined the 1.5 billion dollar failure of the government funded abstinence only programs. Two young adults gave moving testimony on how the abstinence only programs had failed them. Public health expert, John Santelli, M.D., M.P.H., cited numerous independent studies, some federally funded, that have concluded that abstinence only programs are ineffective in preventing teen-age sexual activity and in teaching them to make responsible health decisions. Our young people need truthful, comprehensive education in how best to care for their bodies, in order to prevent disease and unwanted pregnancy.

Birth Control Methods

The most popular choice is **hormonal birth control,** especially the birth control pill. The "Go Ask Alice" website from Columbia University had this to say about how birth control pills work:

> Birth control pills prevent pregnancy through several mechanisms, mainly by stopping ovulation. If no egg is released, there is *nothing to be fertilized by sperm*, [emphasis mine] and the woman cannot get pregnant. Most birth control pills contain synthetic forms of two female hormones: estrogen and progestin. These synthetic hormones stabilize a woman's natural hormone levels, and prevent estrogen from peaking mid-cycle. Without the estrogen bump, the pituitary gland does not release other hormones that normally cause the ovaries to release mature eggs ("How Do Birth Control Pills Work?"

There is also a hormonal birth control pill that uses only progestin (the minipill), for women who cannot tolerate estrogen. This pill is not as effective as the pill that uses both estrogen and progestin, and there will be more breakthrough bleeding. These pills must be taken daily. The FDA has approved new brands of birth control pills that allow women to have their "period" only four times a year.

The two kinds of hormonal birth control are available in other forms: the patch, which is applied once a week; and the vaginal ring, inserted once per month. The woman who cannot tolerate estrogen may choose a progestin only, intramuscular shot, given once every three months, an implant, which is a single-rod that can be removed any time, but must be removed at the end of three years; or an intrauterine device (IUD) that prevent pregnancy for five years or more.

In the United States, all hormonal birth control pills and devices are available only by prescription. A woman should consult her doctor or health care provider for information and help in deciding which method would be best for her.

A report from the Mayo Clinic Staff on the morning-after pill, defines it as emergency birth control used to prevent pregnancy *after* a woman has had unprotected sex. The three common brands are: Plan B One-Step, Next Choice, and Ella. If a woman is seventeen or older, the first two are available over the counter, no prescription is needed. If younger then sixteen, or if Ella, is chosen, a prescription is needed.

In addition to helping prevent pregnancy after unprotected sex, the morning-after pill can help prevent pregnancy in two other instances: if a woman has missed a birth control pill, or if her method of birth control has failed. The morning-after pill can prevent pregnancy because conception usually doesn't occur right after sex. It may occur days later, because sperm has to travel through the fallopian tubes until they can reach an egg (provided an egg is there); therefore, the morning-after pill, taken soon after sex, isn't too late to prevent pregnancy. "The morning-after pill does not end a pregnancy that has implanted ("Morning-After Pill"). [It is not the same as RU-486 or the abortion pill, Mifeprex.]

If a woman doesn't want to use a hormonal birth control, she has alternatives.

Barrier methods, such as condoms for males and females, cervical caps, and the sponge, deserve another look and they can be had "over the counter." In addition, the male condom protects against many sexually transmitted diseases (chlamydia, herpes, HIV, gonorrhea and syphilis). At present a health care provider must prescribe the diaphragm and cervical cap ("Alternates to the Pill").

Because condoms are so important in the prevention of disease, future research needs to take more than a cosmetic look at the condom, and develop a material that has more sensitivity to heat and touch, but is at least as strong and effective as latex ("Alternatives").

Research has produced a diaphragm (SILCS) that fits almost all women. It is made of silicon, which is stronger than the traditional latex; the SILCSs diaphragm is also more comfortable and easier to use than the traditional. Developers are hoping that the diaphragm can be used as a delivery method for microbicide gel that could protect women from HIV and other sexually transmitted infections. A woman would only use the diaphragm when she needed protection. The device has been introduced, and accepted by men and women in four continents. Men in the Dominican Republican reported that they enjoyed the sensation of sex more when their partners used the SILCS diaphragm—a very positive report. If a gel, now being used with the diaphragm, proves to be as effective as the traditional diaphragm with spermicidal gel in preventing pregnancy, the data will be part of the application sent to the US Food and Drug Administration ("A New Kind of Diaphragm").

The Roman Catholic Church allows only the **natural family planning (NFP) method**.[19] Variations exist. The Standard Days Method (SDM) relies on a fixed "window" of fertility. To avoid pregnancy, a woman with cycles twenty-six to thirty-two days long, should not have unprotected intercourse between days eight through nineteen of her cycle. Then there is the TwoDay Method. If a woman notices secretions on the current or previous day, she's probably fertile and should not have intercourse if she wishes to avoid pregnancy. No secretions today and yesterday? Then she is not fertile today

There are other NFP methods. In the Ovulation Method, a woman uses her Basal Body Temperature (BBT) to identify her fertile time. Each morning, before any activity, she takes her temperature: the body temperature is lower before ovulation and rises after ovulation.

Symptothermal Method involves noticing changes in secretions, along with changes in the BBT, and the position and feel of the opening to the cervix. All these symptoms identify the woman's fertile time, and if pregnancy is not desired, she should avoid intercourse.

Lastly, there is the Lactational Amenorrhea Method (LAM) A woman is not fertile while she is nursing, thus she cannot become pregnant, provided: 1) menstruation has not resumed, 2) breast feeds exclusively, which means absolutely *no* water, juice, or regular food supplements given to the baby, and 3) baby is less than six months of age. This method is actually the most successful of all the NFP methods.[20]

Herbal contraceptives, often used by indigenous women, deserve serious study, and the Research Institute for Mindanao Culture, Xavier University, has done just that for the Population Center Foundation. A 1984 study in the Philippines, found that many rural women drink Kamias and other herbal mixtures. The choice of herbs over the birth control pill was influenced by religion, ease of obtaining, and lower cost. Herbs were also considered safer than modern methods, with their accompanying side effects (Quijano Nv Jr.).

It's going to be difficult, because living in a patriarchy *is* difficult for women. With Earth's population, however, on a path to hit nine billion by 2050, according to a United Nations projection, and with water shortages, air pollution, and many species becoming extinct, it is necessary for a good quality of life for all, that we reduce our numbers. Women want smaller families, and we know that they prefer quality over quantity. They will do what's right for them, which will turn out to be right for Mother Earth too. But women need to understand their choices and be free to exercise them.

When women have achieved their fundamental right to control their reproduction, we'll find out then how much more than a "baby machine" a woman is. She has a mind, and a heart, and once allowed to use all her gifts, we'll wonder how we ever got along without them. Men and women, working together will put us on the path toward achieving the other fundamental right, the right of everyone on Earth to enjoy life's basic necessities: food, shelter, education, employment, healthcare, and social security.

Conclusion

Every woman has the fundamental human right to control her reproduction: she owns the womb. Unfortunately the Big Three—religion, government, and culture—want to control her.

Family planning, access to truthful information about birth control and the various methods thereof, are an essential part of every woman's healthcare. If a woman chooses to use birth control, it should be free. The birth control pill, the most popular form of contraceptive, does not cause a "mini-abortion"—that is a myth. The pill, however, is only one of many choices.

Of Wombs and Warriors

I recently returned from San Diego where my husband and I attended the Marine Corps graduation of a second grandson.

Just as in the earlier graduation of an older grandson, uniformly displayed rows of uniformly trained and physically fit, uniformly uniformed young males, were about to become United States Marines. But before that pronouncement, we watched precision marching, heard loudly barked orders, and enjoyed wonderful music from the Marine Corps band. The music <u>was</u> wonderful at first, but after sitting on a steel bleacher for what seemed like forever, my backside ached. I wondered if they'd ever get to the graduation! It was as Shakespeare said in *Othello:* "Pride, pomp, and circumstance of glorious war!" In this case, however, it was the "warriors" who were glorious. It was all a bit much.

In spite of the ache in my bottom, my mind questioned the *why* of all the pomp, this showy display, bordering on the boastful. I also noticed the prideful singling out of some men for special honors. Seven men were given the title of "Honor Man;" one of a company, another of a series, and five of their respective platoons. Then there was a "High Shooter" and a "High PFT," whatever that means. The desire to be "King of the Hill" or the "Top Dog" is strongly encouraged. It probably doesn't take much encouraging; I remember that our two sons sought out competition, and always wanted to be the best and to be recognized and rewarded for accomplishment: "Look at me, Mom! Look what I can do….Watch me! Watch me …"

Anytime you have more than one man, or boy, you have the beginning of a hierarchy. History proves this by just thinking of how many of them men have established: religious, political, educational; and of course, military. Ah, yes, the military, where warriors are recognized for what they can do, especially if it's for actions "above and beyond the call of duty." Lives are on the line in this oldest and ultimate competition: war.

Who Controls?

I thought back to my first grandson's graduation. At the time, I was impressed by the ceremony, thinking little of what would come next. Civil War general, William Sherman, said war "is all Hell." That's an apt description of my older grandson's first tour in Iraq. The fighting was fierce, but nothing could compare with the horror he experienced as he picked up the scattered body parts of what was once his buddy. Even though his second tour was better, the horror of the first is still with him, and probably ever will be. I pray this second grandson will not have such a hellish experience.

War may be hell, but many men seem drawn to it, to desire it. Homer in the *Illiad, wrote "Men grow tired of sleep, love, singing and dancing sooner than of war."*

A song in the sixties asks, "what if someone gave a war and no one came?" Assuming Homer is correct about men and war, this could never happen. Men **will** come. War demands bodies, and women deliver, and deliver, and deliver. It's the old law of supply and demand.

Ouch! This bleacher seat really is really uncomfortable.

I looked out at all the soon to be Marines-for-life standing in front of me. I wondered how many were graduating. Let's see, in my grandson's recruit platoon I can count about 80; and with five platoons, I'd guess I'm looking at close to 400. If graduation goes on every week, that's 20,800 new Marines a year. So between my first grandson's graduation and my second grandson's graduation today, around 83,200 young men have become Marines! But wait, Parris Island also has Marine graduation, and maybe other places do too. War sure needs a lot of bodies to fill its ranks. And every one came from a mother laboring to deliver what is demanded.

The pains of labor and delivery are nothing compared to the labor of love expended in raising children to adulthood—wiping their butts; cleaning up vomit; staying up all night when they have a fever; kissing scraped knees to make "it better," and if that won't do it, making a mad dash to the emergency room. All of that, and now they are "warriors," a fancy name for the much harsher "cannon fodder."

Men! Are we women doomed to always labor and deliver our grown children up to the war machine simply because old men crave the gore and glory of war above all things? As long as we live under patriarchal rule, a woman's value lies mainly in the fruit of her womb; therefore, the answer is "Yes." The most women can hope for is that modern men do not take George Pettie's sixteenth-century advice to heart:

> A woman, an ass, and a walnut tree,
> Bring the more fruit, the more beaten
> They be.

The Abortion Dilemma

"The problem is not so much to know the difference between right and wrong, as to decide what is right and what is wrong" (Philosopher Peter Singer).

Abortion used to be a crime, and many would like to see us go back to those days. Perhaps they figure that with all our modern birth control methods, including the morning-after pill, abortion should not be needed. Unfortunately, they are wrong. A new bill has been proposed by anti-choice leaders in Washington, HR 3803, that would ban abortion after twenty weeks regardless of the situation. A woman could be raped or be in danger of losing her life if her pregnancy continues and she would not be able to receive the necessary health care. Even in the case of a "slip up" and a woman unintentionally gets pregnant, she should be the one who decides what to do about it. Abortion must remain a part of a comprehensive health program for women. It is the right thing to do.

Abortion was criminalized in the mid-nineteenth century and decriminalized one hundred years later with the passage of Roe v. Wade in 1973. To get a more complete view of the subject, we will look at the history of abortion in America, briefly touch on religion and abortion, and then survey situations that present women with the abortion dilemma.[21] In so doing, we will come to realize that even in America where birth control and the morning-after pill is available, abortion needs to remain legal.

Working class women in the 1920s did not make a distinction between birth control and abortion, and the Catholic Church's unspoken acceptance of early abortion prior to "ensoulment," was in force until the mid-nineteenth century. In 1869, however, the Catholic Church condemned abortion, except for therapeutic abortion, which the Church later condemned in 1895. Protestant churches, the medical professions, and the nation's laws at that time, all accepted therapeutic abortions. The Jewish tradition, according to Mishnah code, viewed the woman's life as most important, for "her life takes precedence over its life."

Common law during the eighteenth and early nineteenth centuries deemed that early abortion was legal, but illegal after the "quickening"—the feeling of movement by the mother that occurs at about the fourth month of pregnancy. No one, not even the Catholic Church, believed that human life existed prior to the quickening. Common law, therefore, was grounded in the woman's perception of what was going on inside her own body.

Colonial and early nineteenth century women thought of conception as the "blocking" of menstruation, an imbalance of the body that needed to be balanced to restore the menses. The restoration was done at home and in private, using certain herbs. Savin came from Juniper bushes, easily acquired, as they grew wild; it was the most popular aborticide. Other herbs, pennyroyal, tansy, ergot, and Seneca snakeroot, all found in the woods or grown in gardens, were also used. Recipes for use of these herbs could be found in home medical guides. Women regulated their fertility through abortion, and aborticides became a profitable product sold by doctors, pharmacists, and healers

The first laws governing abortions in the United States, according to the finding of James Mohr (quoted by Reagan), were poison control measures designed to protect pregnant women. It is interesting to note that early nineteenth century laws did not punish women for inducing an abortion and did not eliminate the idea of quickening. And they said nothing about growing plants that could induce an abortion. The laws were aimed at the commercialization of abortion producing plants, leaving women with the right to make their own decisions about their pregnancy before quickening.

About this time, the newly organized American Medical Association (AMA) began a campaign to make abortion illegal at any stage of pregnancy. The campaign, in part, grew out of "regular" physicians' hunger for professional power; in particular, they wanted to get rid of the competition from "irregular" healers, such as Homeopaths and midwives (James Mohr). These regular physicians wanted criminal laws passed against abortion. Such laws would solidify their views and give some state control over the practice of medicine.

The antiabortion campaign was basically antifeminist. Women were condemned for "avoiding the self-sacrifice expected of mothers." It was a backlash campaign in response to the nineteenth century women's movement's fight to gain women the right to enter into the regular medical profession. The antiabortion campaign was fighting to keep women out of their medical schools, societies, and hospitals. It was a battle against women becoming physicians.

Laws criminalizing abortion passed in every state by 1880. Exception was made for therapeutic abortion to save a woman's life. Throughout this time, physicians disagreed on the conditions that needed a therapeutic abortion and the methods used to provide them. Law and medicine looked to each other to define the legal criteria allowing abortion. Throughout this period of illegality, women never stopped demanding the right to control their own reproduction.

The antiabortion campaign sought to do away with the concept of quickening. They wanted to discredit a woman's experience of pregnancy and move pregnancy entirely into the medical field, and they succeeded. No longer was the common law concept of quickening valid, and abortion, *at any point,* in a pregnancy was illegal. Some laws even included punishment for women who aborted. There remained one exception: a physician could perform a therapeutic abortion if the woman's life was threatened.

During the time that abortion was illegal in the United States, millions of abortions were provided to women of every race, class, and marital status. Some were "back alley," but more were provided by physicians, defying the law and the AMA. Women could usually find cooperative abortion providers. If a physician refused, they had to fear that they'd be publicly shamed and possibly prosecuted and that the care could be inferior—they might even die, but many were willing to take that chance.

Then the state got into the act. It formed an alliance with the medical profession. The alliance was accomplished by threatening physicians and medical institutions with prosecution and scandal, until the physicians caved in and cooperated. Cooperation meant that from then on, physicians reported to officials the women who were injured or dying because of an illegal abortion. Punishment awaited those women who made it through the procedure with their lives.

By way of the antiabortion campaign, physicians won the right to claim scientific authority to define life and death; they were setting themselves above the authority of religious leaders, as well as above the general public. They, with the state as their partner, could now set reproductive policy. Women would be, basically, forced into maternity.

The alliance between the state and medicine meant that now the law would investigate the women that physicians reported. The very process of investigation punished the women, for they were then shamed by the public exposure if they were guilty or even potentially guilty—all in order to "teach women a lesson."

Then, starting in the 1960's, a mass movement led by physicians and lawyers and joined by women, demanded that abortion be made legal. Their demands were heard.

The power of women's needs affected medicine, law, and the public debate. After one hundred years of criminality, the Supreme Court's 1973 ruling in Roe v. Wade, established a woman's right to have an abortion. This right is now in danger.

According to a report from The Guttmacher Institute, from January to April of 2012, Republicans have introduced *nine hundred and sixteen (*916!) items of legislation striving to limit a woman's right to control her reproduction. Forty-nine states contributed to this number "with various bills geared toward regulating abortion and a women's right to choose." Some states have already passed their own laws (partial list below).

South Dakota expanded its pre-abortion waiting period from 24 hours to 72 hours, and while the woman waits, she's required to get counseling from a crisis center.

> **Utah** and **Virginia** require their health departments to develop new regulations for abortion clinics. **Utah** also revised its abortion refusal clause to allow any hospital employee to refuse to "participate in any way" in an abortion.

> **Mississippi** now requires all school districts to provide "abstinence only" sex education while permitting discussion of contraception only with the state's permission

.

Three topics garner most of the interest of Republican legislators: insurance coverage of abortion; restriction of abortion; and an ultrasound requirement after the pregnancy has advanced to a specific degree (Ezra Grant).

Today's extreme interest in women and reproduction is reminiscent of the 1880's to the 1920's. During that time, waves of immigrants were pouring into America. Birth rates among the white classes were declining. Antiabortionists did not want the large immigrant families, many of them Catholics, to become more numerous than the white Yankees, for fear they'd become politically powerful. Dr. Horatio R. Storer (quoted by Reagan), leader of the medical wing of the antiabortion movement, wanted native born, white Americans to spread "civilization" south and west, not Mexicans, Chinese, Blacks, Indians, or Catholics. White male patriarchy demanded that *maternity be enforced* (emphasis mine) upon white Protestant women (Reagan, p. 11).

> Ed Pilkington writes in "The Guardian": According to the US census bureau, the dominance of non-Hispanic white people, who today account for two-thirds of Americans, will be whittled away, falling steadily to less than half in 2042 and 46% by 2050. In the opposite trajectory, those who describe themselves as Hispanic,

black, Asian and Native American will increase in proportion from about a third now to 54% by 2050.

Do you see what I mean? The push today to make abortion illegal is more than coincidence.

When I wrote about Reagan's history of abortion, above, I mentioned "ensoulment," the point in time when a person is endowed with a soul. In the various religions, wide disagreements exist about this "point in time": some say that a soul enters—or is it" attached"?—at the moment of conception; others when the fetus is able to live independently of the womb; still others, at the formation of the nervous system and brain; and still others believe that the soul enters at the first breath after birth.

Leaving the answer to the question of ensoulment to the various religions, I ask instead: When does the developing individual become a person? Putting it that way has almost as many answers as the ensoulment question, but it is more inclusive. I'm going to cop out and take refuge in Harry Blackman's 1973 court opinion for Roe v. Wade: "We need not resolve the difficult question of when life begins. When those trained in the respective disciplines of medicine, philosophy, and theology are unable to arrive at any consensus, the judiciary, at this point in the development of man's knowledge is not in a position to speculate."

Why Women Choose Abortion

Every year almost 1.2 million American women have an abortion to end a pregnancy (Kelpie Wilson). Most of them do so in order to conserve assets, including their own physical and mental health that lets them take care of the children they already have. The scenario below, or one quite similar is a common one:

She rushed to the bathroom, closed and locked the door, flipped the lid down on the toilet and sat, breathing hard, her heart pounding. She couldn't stand it out there with them another second. Her two oldest were running around the hdining room table, the one pursued flinging chairs in the path

of his pursuer, and all the while, both yelling. The two others, occupied themselves with blocks; one building a tower and the other sitting on the floor sucking her thumb, watching the blocks rising higher and higher and just waiting for the right moment to knock them all down and send her brother into a tantrum. Alone in the bathroom, she could think.

Thank God, some peace and quiet! I thought I'd lose it for a while there...do something I'd regret. I need to calm down and quit all this worrying. She got up, unbuttoned and unzipped her jeans and pulled them and her panties down. For the eighth time that day, she checked for blood: nothing. Oh, no, I can't be pregnant...how late am I? God, you know I can't take another pregnancy. Please, please, let my period start. What will I tell Karl? He's a hard worker but truck drivers don't make very much if they don't own the truck. He's gone a lot. How can I lay this on him? I want him to enjoy being home. He worries enough as it is. I wish we could afford some help so I could get away once in a while and not be such a crab, but we can't afford it. Those kids go through at least twelve half- gallons of milk a week! And now the dentist says the oldest one needs braces. She'll have to do without.

Hey, I can't hear any yelling...it's too quiet. I better check on them...."

People on the outside of the problem don't see the strain on the family that an unplanned pregnancy produces, especially when the family can't afford it. According to breastfeeding counselor Angela White, the average hospital birth costs about $8,000 and prenatal care by a physician, from $1,500 to $3,000. For the fifty million Americans without insurance, this comes to $10,000. Raising the child from infancy through age seventeen is estimated at $200,000 per child (White quoted by Linda Lowen).

Another common reason given for an abortion is contraceptive failure; more than 50% of all women who have an abortion used a contraceptive method during the month they became pregnant (Women's Health).

Preventing the birth of a child with birth defects or severe medical problems, usually discovered during a second trimester, by use of a routine test, is frequently mentioned as a reason for abortion. A pregnancy resulting from rape or incest is another reason a woman will seek an abortion. Last on the "most common" list of why women get abortions, is fear that their health would be endangered if the pregnancy is continued (Women's Health).

Something I didn't know: "Between 20 and 50 percent of all pregnancies end in a natural (spontaneous) abortion where the woman's body for whatever reason—whether it is a genetically malformed embryo or some environmental or even social stress is triggered to abort…" (Wilson). This means that up to half of all *fertilized* eggs die and are lost, usually before the woman even knows she is pregnant; it's nature's way. [If one considers a fertilized egg the point at which life begins and a person is started, a person who possesses a soul, my question is: What happens to those souls?]

News from the United Kingdom may soon be an important tool in cutting down on abortions done after the first trimester, the time when most serious genetic diseases are discovered. British scientists claim that a gene mapping test could tell parents-to be if embryos are affected by almost any inherited disease. The team from London Bridge Centre says that the test could detect any of the 15,000 inherited diseases in weeks. At present clinics can only test embryos before they are implanted in the woman's womb to determine if they carry a particular gene mutation. For example, the gene for cystic fibrosis is found on chromosome 7. The same testing can be carried out on all chromosomes, allowing for multiple gene screening. Dr. Mark Hamilton, chairman of the British Fertility Society, said "We can currently test for several hundred conditions, but the claim is that the spectrum of conditions which could be screened for is enormous" ('"One-Stop" Embryo Test Unveiled').

Who Controls?

Genetic diseases result from mutated genes that cause abnormalities or deficiencies of necessary proteins or enzymes, making tissues or organs dysfunctional. Some of these mutations are spontaneous during the development of the embryo, while others are inherited. Below I've listed the most serious ones, along with a short explanation.

Sickle Cell Anemia

This is a common inherited blood disorder in America, especially among African-Americans. The red blood cells, the carriers of oxygen, are damaged, resulting in a problem with blood circulation. Symptoms make themselves known during the first or second year of life. This disease can lead to strokes and tissue damage (Maja Fiket).

Cystic Fibrosis

This disease used to be a fatal childhood disease in America, especially among Caucasians. With improved treatments and better ways to manage the disease, however, many people with cystic fibrosis now live into adulthood. Cystic Fibrosis affects the glands, making them produce large amounts of thick mucus that clogs ducts and collects in various organs, resulting in serious breathing and digestive problems (Fiket).

Tay-Sachs Disease

This disease is fatal. It occurs most commonly among Ashkenazi Jews, and is caused by the lack of an enzyme needed to break down a fatty substance in the brain cells. This lack leads to a degeneration of the central nervous system. The disease's symptoms—slow development, loss of vision and gradual loss of other functions—show up when the child is about six-months old. The child becomes mentally retarded and usually dies by four years of age (Fiket).

Duchenne Muscular Dystrophy

Boys are most often affected by this disease; it is characterized by a progressive muscular weakness because of a lack of essential muscle-cell protein. The first symptom is loss of the ability to walk between ages eight and fourteen. In time, death may be caused from breathing and heart problems (Fiket).

Fragile X Syndrome

This is an inherited form of mental retardation, result of a defective X chromosome. It is most common and severe in boys who can suffer mental disability, retardation, or autism (Fiket).

Huntington's Disease

Two-hundred and fifty thousand Americans are affected by this disease or are at risk for inheriting it, making it the most common genetic disease. The disease causes deterioration of the brain, slowly affecting the ability to walk, talk and function— symptoms appear between the ages of thirty and fifty. Victims of this disease need constant care. Life expectancy, once this disease starts, is ten to twenty years (the sooner it starts, the shorter the life expectancy). Death usually results from a stroke, an infection, or a forgetting how to swallow and choking (Fiket).

Anencephaly

This condition, the absence of a large part of the brain and skull, is likely caused by the interaction of multiple genetic and environmental factors. Some of these factors have been identified, but many remain unknown. Changes in dozens of genes may influence the risk of anencephaly. The cases occur sporadically, though a small percentage of cases have been reported to run in families; however, there is no definite pattern of inheritance. Anencephaly is one of the most common neural tube defects, defects that affect the tissue that grows into the spinal cord and brain. The condition occurs early in the development of an unborn baby when the upper part of the neural tube fails to close. Why? No one knows. Anencephaly occurs in about one in ten-thousand births. Having one baby with this condition increases the risk of having another with anencephaly. A pregnancy ultrasound can confirm the diagnosis, and there are other tests as well. The condition usually causes death within a few days (A.D.A.M. Medical Encyclopedia).

Any one of the above conditions, especially the last seven, could cause a woman to desire an abortion, and it would be an understandable desire. The situation that I am going to write about now may be difficult for many to understand, but it is real and understandable to the parents. It comes from an essay written by Steven L. Ross, titled "Abortion and the Death of the Fetus."

The pregnancy in question resulted from failed contraception, and the abortion would occur during the earliest stages of pregnancy. Ross prepares his defense for "killing the fetus even where this could be avoided," (meaning the health of the woman is not in danger, and it is assumed that the baby would be healthy if carried to term), by stating "…a woman has the right to terminate a pregnancy even if doing so results in a … death, simply because anyone has a right to terminate any dependency relation he or she has not willingly entered" (p. 240).

If a woman chooses to bring a pregnancy to term, to have a child, she must be anticipating the birth of someone who she will love and who will love her in return—an intimate relationship. If she chooses, on the other hand, to have this child be dead, she is dreading the birth. Only a parent can, legitimately and comprehensibly, care for a fetus or want it dead.

Choosing the first option in anticipation of a loving relationship in the future is the ideal. Some people, however, do not want to be parents; they do not want there to *be* a child that they will fail or succeed in raising. They cannot be satisfied unless the fetus is killed. This seems extremely selfish and heartless. The situation deserves a closer look.

The parent in this case, is a responsible person. If the child were brought to term, she would feel responsible for its care and upbringing, and she doesn't feel able to do that. (Perhaps she is a single mother who is barely making ends meet as it is. If so, Lowan would see a diminished future for her: "… pregnancy occurring at the wrong place, wrong time in a woman's life can have a lifelong effect on her ability to raise a family and earn a living....Less than half of teens who become mothers before age 18 graduate from high school".)

She could consider adoption, but she does not want to shift her responsibility onto adoptive parents, even if they'd be good ones. She feels very strongly that she and not anyone else ought to raise children she brings into the world, and that she ought to do so with the support of the children's biological father. She defines being responsible, the kind of person she wants to be, as a person who has children only when she can raise them herself in a nurturing environment.

If she allowed her child to be adopted, she would always feel that there was a person in the world, one whom she was failing by not being a proper or full parent, and she dreads this feeling of failure. "Abortion for those with these values is best seen," suggests Ross, "as the only means by which they can regain their situation antecedent to pregnancy where there simply was no child and consequently no one with whom to either succeed or fail as a parent" (245).

She knows that she is expected to love her child, but she anticipates failing to have these feelings when such a person comes into existence. She doesn't want it as she ought to. She feels obligated to love, but one cannot be obliged, forced, to love. Besides, the fetus is not a person any more than "an acorn is an oak tree" [Ross' comparison], but it is more than a potential, in that it is potentially *her* child; she is the only one who has a reason to see the fetus dead. Parents usually intensely desire a potential person to reach maturity. They hope that they will have *their child* and raise him or her in such a way that they pass on their moral values by interacting and being involved with their child's life in an intimate relationship. The biological tie makes them want to mold and nourish the personality of *their* child. "Only when we hold fast to the way an ongoing and uniquely binding relationship looms large from the start with this rapidly dividing group of cells, do we provide the ground for a real concern and for a satisfactory defense of abortion" (p. 248).

I quoted Ross at the beginning of this argument, "…a woman has the right to terminate a pregnancy even if doing so results in a…death, simply because anyone has a right to terminate any dependency relation he or she has not willingly entered." Not only is it her right, it is her decision because she is the one who will undergo the operation.

Peter Singer, philosopher and professor of bioethics, would agree. In his book, *Writings on an Ethical Life,* he suggests rewriting The Commandments. He would rewrite "Be Fruitful and Multiply," to read, "Bring children into the world only if they are wanted."

He explains: "There are (or soon will be) as many people on this planet as it can reasonably be   expected to support. If it is not wrong to kill an embryo because of the wrong it does to an existing being, then the fact that killing it will mean that one fewer person comes into existence does not make it wrong either. "

Kelpie Wilson too is concerned about the growth of population and the physical limits of Planet Earth. Humans have a long history of attempts to avoid starvation by regulating population growth. "Pro-life" could means, regulating population in order to *save* lives.

"Human life and civilization are now deeply threatened by resource depletion, toxic pollution and climate catastrophe. Already shortages of food, fuel and water are making it difficult to meet the basic needs of the 6.5 billion people on the planet and no one has any idea how we will feed the 9.1 billion people projected to be here by 2050" (Wilson).

Conclusion

Enough of this "turn off the baby machine," then "turn on the baby machine," rigmarole, Control of reproduction belongs by right in the hands of women. Another important right is the right to health care, and a comprehensive health care program for women must include family planning, with abortion available if needed.

Who Controls?

Before the middle of the nineteenth century, abortion was legal in America, but after that time, it was illegal for about one hundred years, the illegality ending with the Supreme Court ruling in Roe v. Wade (1973). In spite of the illegality, millions of women, of every race, class, and marital status, were determined to abort their pregnancies, and they succeeded.

Now this right is in danger. It may be because by the year 2050 white Americans will be in the minority at 46% of the population, with Hispanic, Black, Asian and Native Americans making up 54% of the population. The potential loss of political power throws some people into a panic.

Women choose abortion for a variety of reasons—economic and medical being most common. Most abortions are done in the first trimester.

It is a woman's right to end a dependency relationship that occurred against her will and that she does not want.

Who's Your Mama?

In the movie, *Chicago,* the prison matron, Mama Morton (played by Queen Latifah), sings to the inmates: "When you're good to Mama, Mama's good to you."

We are all prisoners on Mother Earth, and we have nowhere else to go. Mother Earth nourishes us as surely as a human baby is nourished at the mother's breast: Mother Earth is everything to us.

Some call Mother Earth "Gaia," the name given her by the ancient Greeks, embodying what we mean when we say "Mother Earth," the nurturer of all. She also has a dark side: "Like Kali [the Hindu goddess], Gaia was gentle, feminine and nurturing, but also ruthlessly cruel to any that crossed her" (Chamberlin. "The Gaia Hypothesis")

James Lovelock, in the mid-60s, hypothesized that the Earth was a living object, having the attributes of a living thing—the ability to undergo chemical processes by which to sustain life and regenerate damaged parts.[22]

James B. Irwin, Apollo 15, saw the Earth from the spacecraft and thought it a "beautiful, warm living object." He also thought it looked "so fragile, so delicate, that if you touched it with a finger it would crumble and fall apart." Lovelock would not agree that the Earth is fragile and delicate. He sees the Earth as strong—able to withstand the destructive force "as [humankind] befouls and cripples the bio-dynamics of its environment." After all, she has withstood an asteroid collision of great magnitude. He adds, however, that the "passage of a bullet is also momentary, but the damage nonetheless lethal…human caused imbalance, at a critical juncture, might be catastrophic to Gaia" (S. Miller). What is catastrophic to Gaia/Earth is catastrophic to all living things.

Self-preservation is of utmost importance to all living things, and that includes Mother Earth. In our misguided and overzealous efforts to "subdue" her, we have hurt her badly and are continuing to do so. We rape her resources; suffocate her by removing her "lungs," if you will—the forests that take in our carbon dioxide and give off oxygen; kill off species of animals that form her senses[23]; scar her with explosives; destroy her kidneys by draining her marshes; befoul her rivers and oceans with poisonous chemicals; and burn her with radioactive waste. You can probably think of other injuries to our Mother Earth. We have definitely NOT been good to Mama. What happens when she won't take it anymore?

We are Earth's prisoners, and we have been her dependents since the beginning of our existence. We are trapped; we have nowhere else to go. It's time, right now, to forget about our human differences and to work together to clean up our act. We must start being good to Mama by caring for her before she takes care of us—for good.

Many of us, especially those of us with an economic stake in "business as usual," are in denial about the serious consequences of the mess we've made on Mother Earth—the climate changes that have begun and will only get worse, the pollution that fouls her air and her waters, the imminent depletion of her resources by the sheer weight and demands of the human mass. Those that continue to deny, will find out that the laws of chemistry and physics are immutable and can not be denied.

Granted, climate science has its uncertainties, and scientists don't always agree. The unusually hot summer of 1988 may just have been Mother Earth having a hot flash. But in that summer, NASA climatologist James Hansen told Congress that he was '99 percent' certain that a "long-term warming trend had begun, probably caused by the greenhouse effect." Some began to be concerned about fossil-fuel emissions (Mooney 42).

Even after the report by the Intergovernmental Panel on Climate Change (IPCC), formulated by experts, came out in 1990, the issue of global warming was still open to reasonable doubt. The IPCC's second report, completed in 1995, concluded that in addition to natural factors, human beings were also affecting the climate.

Who Controls?

In 2001, the IPCC's third report came out. It showed a strong consensus, rare in science, about its findings: "Notwithstanding some role for natural variability, human-created greenhouse gas emissions could, if left unchecked, ramp up global average temperature by as much as 5.8 degrees Celsius (or 10.4 degrees Fahrenheit) by the year 2100" (Mooney).

Now the fourth IPCC report (2007) is out, superseding all previous reports. It definitely fingers humans as being a *major* part of the problem: "Warming of the climate system is unequivocal", and "most of the observed increase in global average temperatures since the mid-20th century is very likely due to the observed increase in anthropogenic greenhouse gas concentrations."

Carbon dioxide emissions are raising the levels of acidity in the world's oceans to such a degree that, even if we try, we will not be able to reverse acidity levels in our lifetime. And they are predicted to keep rising. The first to suffer will be the tiny, shelled plankton, food source for fish and other animals. As the acidity increases, it will become harder for marine life to breathe and reproduce. In addition, the chemical changes in the oceans will cut down on their ability to absorb carbon dioxide from the atmosphere, causing the rate of global warming to speed up ("Emission Cuts").

Mother Earth is not like the Old Woman who lives in a shoe; Mother Earth knows what to do, and she is powerful.

In the 1330s, an outbreak of bubonic plague erupted in China, a busy trading nation. In October of 1347, Italian merchant ships carried the plague to Sicily. The disease killed with incredible speed. The Italian writer Boccaccio said its victims 'ate lunch with their friends and dinner with their ancestors in paradise. By August of 1348, the killer plague had spread across Europe and was in England. Within five years, 25 million people, one-third of Europe's people, were dead (Rice). Modern plagues will not be spread via slow moving merchant ships. With air travel, they zoom throughout the world.

Who Controls?

Looking at just the twentieth century, the worldwide flu epidemic of 1917 managed to kill twenty million people (including my grandfather). Five other epidemics occurred from 1907 to 1920, killing a little over ten million more, making a grand total of over thirty million people killed by twentieth century epidemics ("The Most Deadly 100"). Add to that total the twenty million people in the world who died of AIDS between1981 to 2003 ("World HIV & AIDS"), and epidemics have killed over fifty million. Other, less severe, natural disasters in the twentieth century have killed millions of the world's people--famines killing almost seven million, floods killing more than five and one-half million, and droughts killing about the same number as floods ("The Most Deadly").

Taken all in all, the twentieth century was pretty deadly; the twenty-first century could be deadlier. Scientists are calling on rich nations to help fight bird flu, or "risk a global flu pandemic.[24]" Asia, Europe, and Africa are doing the best they can to contain outbreaks among domestic and wild birds, fearing the development of an Avian [Bird] Flu that would be easily transmitted to humans. At present, an Avian Flu virus, H5N1, has a human mortality rate of sixty percent ("H5N1").

Rich nations need to pay attention, as a pandemic would cause "enormous economic dislocation. Stock markets will close; international travel and trade will be limited." If the virus should infect someone carrying human flu, and a hybrid germ develops, the flu death toll could be in the tens of millions (Kent, "Bird Flu"). A pandemic of any kind that kills millions would have one—dare I say "positive" effect? It would slow the rate of global warming

It is predicted that by the year 2050, our population will be about nine billion ("Three Billion More"). The changes in climate and our increasing numbers—will lead us to make our homes in less desirable areas, making all of these disaster totals escalate. Sea levels have risen five to eight inches over the past 100 years, making it dangerous to live on or near beaches (Cline, "Population and Natural Disasters"). On December 26, 2004 a gigantic wall of water, a tsunami, smashed into and over the lands around the Indian ocean, killing at least 200,000 people in no time at all ("Tsunami Aid").

Cline predicts "Rising sea levels in the coming decades will make such waves even more destructive." It is not only the rising sea levels that are to blame, dynamite fishing has destroyed coral reefs and mangroves have been cut and filled for development; both of which used to slow down fast-moving waves, according to Jeff McNeely, of the World Conservation Union ("Population and Natural Disasters"). If the 2004 tsunami was a bitter taste of what living without concern for what ecology can bring, the 2005 Hurricane Katrina was an angry, vicious bite, chewing up the United States' Gulf Coast. Is Mother Earth trying to tell us something?

Has she, perhaps, had enough of our destruction and abuse? We have abused her frightfully. Could she be trying to get rid of us once and for all? If so, we are on a course heading for more of Mother Nature's natural disasters and more human tragedy.

Epidemics did the best job of decreasing our numbers, but our big brains have now produced vaccines, inoculations, antibiotics, etc., that have drastically cut the number of deaths by disease. Not even the brutal, atrocious things we do to each other can kill enough people to reach sustainability. [*Sustainability* is the ability to meet our present needs without endangering the ability of our descendants to meet their needs.]

I wanted to know how efficient mankind was when it came to killing. Below are listed the "Source List and Detailed Death Tolls for the Primary Mega deaths of the Twentieth Century":

Second World War	66 million killed
Joseph Stalin	20 million killed
First World War	15 million killed
Russian Civil War	9 million killed
People's Republic of China: Zedong's regime)	40 million killed (Mao

In 1994 it took only one hundred days to murder almost one million people in the genocidal war between the Hutus and the Tutsis ("Rwanda: A Brief History"). Another genocidal war in the Darfur region of Sudan has killed at least 300,000, according to UK-based Dr. Jan Coebergh, who once worked in Darfur. He adds, "We don't know enough about how many people are dying from violence let alone natural causes in inaccessible areas."

Wars are efficient in reducing population; especially high marks go to the Second World War. Since then we've developed more effective weapons. Raytheon Missile Systems, with Bofors Defense of Sweden, developed the **M982 Excalibur** (previously **XM982**), a 155 mm extended range guided artillery shell. The missile can hit targets twenty-five miles away, more than twice the distance of a conventional artillery shell. We're making progress in devising killing tools, but no matter how much we reduce our population numbers, the reductions don't last. We are just too fertile for our own, and Mother Earth's, good

How We Damage Gaia

Margaret Mead stated the obvious: "We won't have a society if we destroy the environment." A balance must be reached between human demand, Earth's capacity to supply and also her ability to absorb, our noxious emissions. We must strive for sustainable society, but first, let's look at the damage that's been done to our beloved Earth.

A study, actually an audit of nature's economy, done by the Millennium Ecosystem Assessment over a period of four years by 1,300 researchers from ninety-five nations, does just that. The report says, "The way society obtains its resources has caused *irreversible* [Emphasis added] changes that are degrading the natural processes that support life on Earth." This degradation by mismanagement has occurred over the last fifty years (Amos).

A post World War II baby boom spurred the rush to use natural resources. "More land was converted to agriculture since 1945 than in the 18th and 19th centuries combined. More than half of all the synthetic nitrogen fertilizers ever—first made in 1913---

used on the planet were deployed after 1985." Fisheries and fresh water cannot sustain current demands, let alone those of the future. We need to severely reduce the use of such natural resources if we hope to make any progress in alleviating poverty, eradicating hunger, and improving health (Amos, "Study Highlights"). Nowhere is this truer than in Africa.

The Working Group on Climate Change and Development titled their report, "Africa: Up in Smoke?" It calls for "deeper" emission cuts in rich countries and for funding to help poor countries cope with global warming. Africa is predicted to be the hardest hit by the effects of global warming because of its dependence upon rain for crop production. Africans must address the issue of climate change and how to adapt to it, or poverty will inevitably increase (Briggs).

Without water no life can exist, and the Earth will soon be facing a serious water shortage. ZPG, the Population Connection, reports that only 0.3 percent of the world's water is available for human use; 40 percent of the Earth's ground water is contaminated, due largely to mismanagement ("Population and the Environment"). *BBC NEWS* (online) of March 22, 2001 warns of a coming water shortage by 2025, at which time "Two people in three across the world will face water shortages" (Kirby, 'World Warned").

When Americans think of hunger, they usually think of famine. That's not necessarily so. Many people live in countries with enough food, but either it's too expensive for them to buy, or the country is in such political turmoil that it is simply too difficult to get. People moving from the country to the city often experience hunger. They are no longer able to grow their own food and many times they do not earn enough money to buy the food they need.

Jonathan Amos, "Earth's Species Feel the Squeeze," reminds us that a strong link exists between species extinction and poverty; people depend on fish, mammals, and birds for food. World Wildlife Fund's (WWF) recent report tells us that biodiversity is down 30% since the 1970s, with tropical species declining the most. We, however, are flourishing and outstripping Mother Earth's resources by 50%--using the resources of one and one half Earths a year (2012 Living Planet Report). Colby Loucks, director of conservation sciences at WWF, kindly said that we are "bad houseguests." He explained: "We're emptying the fridge, we're not really taking care of the lawn, we're not weeding the flower beds and we're certainly not taking out the garbage."

The destruction of our forests at record rates and the burning of fossil fuels increase the emission of global greenhouse gases like carbon dioxide. Our weather patterns are affected by this; they've become more erratic. Because of the damaging storms in the United States, homeowners and motorists should expect a rise in insurance costs. Ian Crowder, a spokesman for AAS Insurance said that there wouldn't be a huge increase in premiums, but the cost of building insurance would rise as insurers expect "extreme weather" conditions to increase in frequency

Of all the bad things done or being done to our planet, not make me sadder than the condition of the river Ganges. It receives 1.1 million liters of raw sewage EVERY MINUTE, according to the World Health Organization (WHO). The make-up of this raw sewage is alarming, "One gram of feces can contain ten million viruses, one million bacteria, 1,000 parasite cysts and one hundred worm eggs." This toxic mix is particularly harmful to children because of their low body weight, lack of relative strength, and their ignorance of sanitary measures that could protect them (Kirby, "Global Sewage."

The Dalai Lama spoke to the problem of **too many people** in his Millennium Message on January 1, 2000. "One of the greatest challenges today is the population explosion." Too many exist for this one Earth. To provide us with resources and to absorb all of our noxious emissions, we would need more than one and one-fifths Earth's (Donella Meadows, Randers, and Dennis Meadows, 31). As no other Earth is in sight, we *must* decrease our numbers before Earth does it for us.

This is the way the world ends

Who Controls?

> Not with a bang but a whimper.
> T. S. Eliot: *The Hollow Men*

Eliot may be wrong; it may yet end with a bang. There is always a war—or two or three or more--going on in the world. Humans are aggressive, and aggression can be addicting:

> As a popular form of arousal… [aggression]… rivals sex. It invigorates. It gives a sense of well-being and increased stature; it is immediately emotionally rewarding. It can be secondarily rewarding, too, because people who behave aggressively tend to get more of their own way than people who don't. (Morgan, 198)

What's not to like? Men and women who have experienced the rewards of aggression try to find situations that will again arouse these feelings, or they will think about them, all so that "delicious shot of adrenalin will once more flow through their veins" (Morgan 198).

"War," continues Morgan, "is a function of male bonding (204)…a kind of love, and of a high order because it produces deeds of devotion and self-sacrifice, and trust and obedience so unqualified that even the power of independent thought is sacrificed on its altar" (199). Unable to think independently, male bonding can turn men into a mindless mob, firing up each other to commit murder and mayhem. Women can hate the enemy as much as a man, and fight for their families and even property, but they do not bond as men do. They do not lose the ability to think independently (203).

If only men could fight their wars without dragging women and children into it, but that's impossible; besides, raping women and girls is one of the spoils of war. Our big brains have enabled us to device weapons of mass destruction. According to a Federation of American Scientists update, on the 7th of May 2012 there were approximately 19,000 nuclear warheads in the world. We certainly have enough weapons power to die with a BANG

Mother Earth Fights Back

The thousands killed in Europe's "Extreme Summer" of 2003 (Dickinson), and the 200,000 killed by the tsunami of 2004, may have been a warning. Mother Earth has had enough of our destruction. Rising sea levels could drown up to two billion people within the next fifty years as floods ravage islands and coastal areas. Usually the poorest people are most at risk ("World Faces"). The whole world witnessed that truth after Hurricane Katrina struck in 2005.

Lest you shrug off the idea of floods as just a scare tactic of "tree huggers," let's looks at the statistics: six major flood disasters in the 1950s, seven in the 1960's, eight in the 1970's, 18 in the 1980's and 26 in the 1990's ('World Faces"). In 2010 we hit the jackpot with thirteen major flood disasters with more than twenty-one million affected and thousands killed. If governments fail to cut emissions of carbon and fail to improve the defense of coastlines, the worldwide cost of storms will escalate by about two-thirds ("Storm Cost"). Climate change brings extremes in weather. The Gulf Coast of the United States now knows that well.

In the United States, more than 80 percent of the population lives in cities. The United Nations predicts it is only a matter of months before half of all humans will be city dwellers. Developing countries, where a billion people now live in "shanty towns," are the ones that will see essentially all the urban growth in the next twenty-five years, putting a severe strain on their ability to provide resources and services (D. Whitehouse). As the world becomes ever more urban, Mother Earth will find it easier to get rid of us—we'll be all "bunched up."

The Road to Worldwide Sustainability

We know what's coming; we see the writing on the wall. The longer we wait the more sacrifice it will take. Our goal: worldwide sustainability to save not only us, animal species, but perhaps our Mother Earth as well.

Couples will be encouraged to have no more than two children, an ideal that calls for effective, free birth control for all who want it. All of the things we do to reach sustainability will accomplish nothing if human fertility is not decreased (Donella Meadows, Randers, and Dennis Meadows, 37).

Limit industrial output to provide an adequate, but not excessive, standard of living for all. (Industry eats up enormous amounts of energy.) "Fossil Fuel Subsidies 'Must End'" writes Alex Kirby, reporting on the conclusion of a United Kingdom think-tank: "The only way to meet international poverty targets is by a massive switch to renewable energy, can we hope to end poverty …"

Develop technologies to decrease pollution of all kinds, including pollutants produced by aviation and shipping. Aviation,[25] in particular, is of concern because it uses a lot of fuel at high altitudes ("Aviation"). This means finding viable alternatives for fossil fuel, thus decreasing pollutants. The use of fossil fuels pollutes the spirit: "Around the world control of fossil fuels is linked to corruption and violence" (Simms quoted in Kirby, "Fossil Fuel Subsidies").

Technology is crucial in our fight, but the costs of technology must be kept down. At all times, cost effectiveness must be a prime concern to avoid bankrupting a society. Great technology combined with cost effectiveness to stop and reverse all pollution will challenge our best brains.

Increase land yield and protect agricultural land will be a priority, but we must do this in such a way that we do not pollute our water resources. Organic farming needs to be encouraged. Crucial to success is the curtailment of the urban sprawl that is gobbling up good farmland. Build up rather than out as a fashionable and attractive alternative.

Plant more trees. Plant trees wherever possible, on islands between traffic lanes, in backyards, even on rooftops!

Fostering the Will to Cooperate

In serving each other, we become free (Camelot).

No hope of cooperation between peoples exists if some universal truths about human nature are not taken into account.[26]

1. We are social beings, concerned about our relatives. If we look back far enough, we are all relatives. "The existence of African Eve, our common mother, is extremely likely because the genetic material of all humans alive today is eerily similar" (Shlain, 7). Therefore, we should all be concerned about all of us.

2. We readily cooperate in reciprocal relationships. Never has cooperation been needed more; but, being human, we need to know "What's in it for me?" Until people become committed to serving each other, we'll need to provide incentives to make them want to work for the common good.

3. Humans [especially men] form hierarchies. Hierarchies based on economics lead to greed and corruption. That is not to say that all hierarchies are bad. The Boy Scouts used a hierarchical system to bring out the best in young boys. We can turn this proclivity into a positive trait if the hierarchy is based on altruism and heroism. People want recognition and appreciation; let's give it to them for life-enhancing reasons.

4. Men are more involved in physical conflict than are women. Wars are getting just too destructive In the United States, 94 percent of prisoners are males. As far as teen crime goes, between the years 1988 and 1992, there was a 300 percent increase in the number of teen murderers (Stephenson 2, 33).

Fewer boys are being born in the United States. Usually more boys than girls are born (probably to compensate for the higher death rate in boys). After 1942, however, the sex ratio started to change. There are now 850,000 fewer males than there would have been had the sex ratio stayed at 1942 rates (R. Knox,).

5. Women are more involved in childcare than are men. This is changing, perhaps because families are becoming smaller. Children benefit immensely by having "daddy" around more, and so do we. Testosterone (the hormone fueling aggression), levels are not as high in good fathers (Abrams).

Countries are busily developing and expanding market economies. It is thought that this fosters initiative and hard work. But money, materialism, can't buy happiness, and happiness is more important. Enough is plenty. What we really need is "to encourage a broader sense of self-interest, in which we seek to build on the social and cooperative side of our nature rather than the individualistic and competitive side." Most people will respond positively to a genuine and mutually beneficial form of cooperation (Singer, 279-282).

There will always be competition, but we can find ways to channel it to the benefit of society, and promote social structures that stress cooperation over competition. Cooperative people encourage others to cooperate, and a "virtuous" spiral ensues because cooperation produces the best payoffs (Singer 280-1) If we must have some competition, how about a contest to figure out the best way to foil those who try to game the system?

Who Controls?

People are moving away from family farms to urban areas. Cities are getting so big, so filled with strangers, that it's hard to get people to cooperate with each other: Feelings of anonymity and alienation must somehow be overcome so that people will work together. Outcasts see no reason to cooperate—why should they? Therefore, the economic conditions producing outcasts must first be eliminated in a society desiring cooperation (Singer 280-1).

It is vital that all work together to stop global warming, and "therein lies the rub." Not only love of competition stands in our way. We are a fractious species, addicted to aggression, and too often we hate and fear each other. We can no longer afford our prejudices. Very young children are tolerant, but learn to be intolerant very quickly.

> You've got to be taught to hate and fear
> You've got to be taught from year to year
> It's got to be drummed in your dear little ear
> You've got to be carefully taught.
> --"South Pacific" by Rodgers and
> Hammerstein

Parents, talk to your children and teach tolerance of religion, race, ethnicity, and gender. A couple of quotations to keep you focused:

> Do not unto others what you would not have them do unto
> you
> --Confucius

> We must all hang together or we will all hang separately.
> --Benjamin Franklin

Conclusion

Mother Earth, is strong, but even the strong can be vulnerable; can have an "Achilles heel." Our actions toward her and toward each other have put all in danger of extinction.

We must to treat our home, our beloved planet, with gentleness and respect before she decides we aren't worth the trouble anymore.

Sustainability is our life-saving goal, and to achieve it we must start by putting the brakes on our fertility. Fewer people will reduce the size of all our problems. If we fail to reduce our numbers, all other steps taken to preserve ou4 planet and to combat climate change will be futile.

Paul Simon reminds us that we are all in this together as we face danger, by his song, "Citizen of the Planet." As Earth's citizens, we have a right to demand that our leaders hear our voices.

We are the citizens of the planet
We were born here
We're going to die here

Endnotes:

[1] About 150,000 years ago, postulates Shlain, "some yet-to-be-identified event occurred that allowed the survival of [a] particular group of hominids. From this stressed band a single female known as Mitochondrial African Eve succeeded [in] giving birth to the new species…Homo sapiens…" (5-7).

[2] Shlain has observed during his years of medical practice that men in general are more afraid of death than are women (271).

[3] We now know that a child growing up without a father is "at greater risk for everything from school failure to teen suicide" (Lamb). Canadian studies found that while testosterone may drive a man to sire a child, other hormones kick in to turn a stud into a good father (Abrams).

[4] Times have not changed for all. In Afghanistan today, "It is said women are traded like commodities to settle debts and disputes and that some women commit suicide to escape being forced into unwanted marriages" ("Group Cites"). Further, "Women all over Afghanistan are still being murdered, raped and imprisoned with impunity, according to Amnesty International ("Afghan Women").

[5] Sociology professor, Hans-Peter Kohler of the University of Pennsylvania, found that people with children are happier than those without; however, having more than one child did not increase their happiness (Krakovsky).

[6] Table 2. All Races, Percent Childless.

[7] In addition to natural brain differences, his child bride's brain has probably been affected by her brutal treatment. Physical endangerment causes mental trauma, affecting the ability to learn. Fear actually alters the pathways of the brain, hindering logical thought (Dowling 148-9).

[8] In an experiment with one-hundred dollar bills falling from above, boys were able to catch six bills while girls caught none ("Science of the Sexes").

[9] Nyborg, H. 1994. *Hormones, Sex, and Society.* Westport, Conn: Praeger.

[10] "World Divorce Statistics,"

[11] With the dramatic changes over the past years, never-married men have narrowed the health gap between themselves and married men; however, there is still a gap. People who had been married in the past and were now widowed or divorced experienced declines in their overall health status.

[12] Sung by the Righteous Brothers, music and lyrics by Barry Mann, Cynthia Weil, and Philip Spector.

[13] Wright says that women usually prefer older partners

[14] Department of Anthropology Wheaton College, Wheaton, Illinois

[15] *Good News Bible*. Genesis 38:9.

[16] An overpopulated state, however, with many people at the poverty level is a state in trouble. Now numbers are not giving strength, they are draining the state of resources, perhaps to the brink of bankruptcy, or the people may rebel and seek to overthrow the state, should their numbers and their misery be great enough.

[17] Information about Margaret Sanger was found in Deborah F. Felder's book, *The 100 Most Influential Women of All Time.*

[18] , In 2008, the CDC reported a rise in the teen birthrate for the first time in sixteen years

[19] In January of 2009, L'Obsservatore Romano, the Vatican newspaper, came out with a report saying "the contraceptive pill is polluting the environment and is in part responsible for male infertility. Gianbenedetto Melis, vice-resident of a contraceptive research association, told ANSA news agency: "Once metabolized, the hormones contained in oral contraceptives no longer have any of the characteristic effects of feminine hormones."

[20] All NFP information here comes from "New Simpler Methods of Natural Family Planning."

[21] All material detailing the history of abortion in America was gleaned from Leslie J. Reagan's book, *When Abortion Was a Crime.*

[22] James Lovelock called his first proposal the *Gaia hypothesis*. But the term established nowadays is *Gaia theory*. Lovelock explains that the initial formulation was based on observation, but still lacked a scientific explanation. The Gaia Hypothesis has since been supported by a number of scientific experiments and provided a number of useful predictions, and hence is properly referred to as the Gaia theory. In fact, wider research proved the original hypothesis wrong, in the sense that it is not life alone but the whole Earth system that does the regulating. Viewed 17 May 2012<http://en.wikipedia.org/wiki/Gaia_hypothesis

[23] "The inner workings of Gaia ... can be viewed as a study of the physiology of the Earth, where the oceans and rivers are the Earth's blood, the atmosphere is the Earth's lungs, the land is the Earth's bones, and the living organisms are the Earth's senses ("The Gaia Hypothesis," 4).

[24] "Science Journal Could Give Recipe for Deadly Avian Flu Virus." Libby Lewis, CNN Radio, 12 May 2012. The "recipe" comes from an experiment by a Dutch scientist who engineered the avian [bird] flu virus to make it airborne and thus deadlier to mammals. The U. S. government funded the experiment, and scientists are in debate over the possible results.

Who Controls?

Dr. Anthony Fauci, head of the NIH agency funding infectious disease research says, "We need as scientists and health officials to stay one step ahead of the virus as it mutates and changes its capability."

Dr. Thomas Inglesby, Center for Biosecurity at the University of Pittsburgh Medical Center, states, "We are playing with fire."
Viewed 17 May 2012
<http://www.10news.com/health/31055197/detail.html>
[25] Aviation is not even mentioned in the Kyoto agreements.
[26] The first sentence in each of the following numbered items was taken from Peter Singer's book, *Writings on an Ethical Life,* (276-277).

Bibliography

ABRAMS, DOUGLAS CARLTON. "Father Nature: The Making of a Modern Dad. *"Psychology Today*. Mar. /Apr. 2002: 38-47.

"Afghan Women 'Still Suffer Abuse.'" *BBC News* 30 May 2005 <http://news.bbc.co.uk/1/hi/world/south_asia/4592697.stm>

"Alternatives to the Pill." 01 Jan 06. 19 May 12 <http://www.oprah.com/relationships/Beyond-the-Pill_1/8>

"Americans for Divorce." *Divorce Reform.*20 Dec. 2004 <http://www.divorcereform.org/lea.html>

AMOS, JONATHAN. "Study Highlights Global Decline." *BBC News* 30 Mar.2005 <http://news.bbc.co.uk/1/hi/sci/tech/4391835.stm>

ANGELOU, MAYA. "I Know Why the Caged Bird Sings." *The Poetry of Maya Angelou*. 6 Oct. 2004 <http://www.empirezine.com/spotlight/maya/maya-p2.htm#caged%20bird>

"Anencephaly." A.D.A.M. Medical Encyclopedia. 01 May 11. 13 Jun 12 <http://www.ncbi.nlm.nih.gov/pubmedhealth/pmH0002547/>

ARMAS, GENARO C. "Men, Women in No Hurry to Marry, Census Reveals." Arizona Daily Star 2 Dec. 2004: A1, A15.

."Study: A Record 44% of Women 15-44 Childless." Arizona Daily Star 25 Oct. 2003: A1.

"Aviation 'Huge Threat to CO2 Aim." BBC News. 20 Sept. 2005 <http://news.bbc.co.uk/1/hi/sci/tech/4266466.stm>

BLACKMUN, JUSTICE HARRY. 29 Jun 12 <http://choice101.com/42-roe-v-wade.html>

BRIGGS, HELEN. "Warming Link' to Big Hurricanes." BBC News. 16 Sept. 2005
<http://news.bbc.co.uk/1/hi/sci/tech/4249138.stm>

BROWN, LESTER. "World in the Balance." Interview by Sarah Holt. NOVA 17 Jan. 2005
<http://www.pbs.org/wgbh/nova/worldbalance/voic-brow.html>

BROWNING, ROBERT. "Rabbi Ben Exra." *The Norton Anthology of English Literature.* (Rev. Vol. 2). Ed. M.H. Abrams, et al. New York: Norton, 1968.

CAHN, SAMMY. "Love and Marriage." Wedding Vendors. 29 Dec. 2004
<http://www.weddingvendors.com/music/lyrics/song0237.html>

_____."The Tender Trap." Song Lyrics 4 U. 8 Dec. 2004
<http://www.songlyrics4u.com/frank-sinatra/tender-trap.html>

CHAMBERLIN, SEAN. "The Gaia Hypothesis." 17 May 12
http://www.bibliotecapleyades.net/gaia/esp_gaia01.htm

Psychology "Children Need Fathers, Study Shows." Divorce Reform. 16 Dec. 2004 <http://patriot.net/~crouch/adr/kids.html>

Cline, Tim. "Population and Natural Disasters." The Reporter. Spring 2005: 19.

_____."Population Matters: Now More Than Ever." The Reporter. Spring 2004:19-24.

DICKINSON, TIM. "Diary of a Dying Planet." Rolling Stone 10 June 2004:76-81.

DOUGHERTY, TIM, AND LILLIAN KUROSAKA. "Study Finds Teen Pregnancy and Crime Levels Are higher Among Kids from Fatherless Homes." Press release11 Oct. 1996. Divorce Reform. 16 Dec. 2004 <http://patriot.net/~crouch/adc/jds.html>

DOWLING, COLETTE. *The Frailty Myth: Women Approaching Physical Equality.* New York: Random, 2000.

ELST, KOANRAAD. "4.1 Islam Condoning Birth Control." 23 May 12 <http://www.koenraadelst.voiceofdharma.com/books/demogislam/part4.html>

"Emission Cuts 'Vital' for Oceans." BBC News. 1 July 2005 <http://news.bbc.co.uk/1/hi/sci/tech/4633681.stm>

ENGLEMAN, ROBERT. "More Choice for Women Means More Sustainability." Worldwatch Institute. 07 May 08. 07 Jun 12 < http://www.worldwatch.org/5737>

"Europe Tackles 'Honour Killings.'" BBC News 22 June 2004. 9 July 2005 <http://news.bbc.co.uk/2/hi/world/europe/3828675.stm>

FELDER, DEBORAH F. *The 100 Most Influential Women of All Time: A Ranking Past and Present*. New York: Carol Publishing Group, 1996.

FIKET, MAJA. "Genetic Childhood Diseases." 13 Jun 12 <http://www.allvoices.com/contributed-news/12335277-5-most-dangerous-hereditary-diseases>

FISHER, HELEN. "Biology." Psychology Today. 10 July w003 <http://www.psychologytoday.com/htdocs/prod/ptoarticle/pto-19930301-000030.asp>

_____.The First Sex: *The Natural Talents of Women and How They Are Changing the World.* New York: Random, 1999.

FOULKES-JAMISON, Ph.D. "The Effects of Divorce on Children."01 Jan 01. 07 May 12 <http://cpancf.com/articles_files/effectsdivorceonchildren.asp

GERSHWIN, IRA. "Love Is Here to Stay." Wedding Vendors. 29 Dec. 2004 <http://www.weddingvendors.com/music/lyrics/song-903.html>

GOOD NEWS BIBLE: TODAY'S ENGLISH VERSION. "Genesis 38:9." New York: American Bible Society, 1976.

GORDON, SERENA. "Married Folks Still the Healthiest." 11 Aug 08. 29 Jun 12 <http://www.washingtonpost.com>

GRANT, EZRA. "Domestic Policies." 20 Apr 11. 06 Jun 12 < http://www.ezkool.com/2011/04/in-four-month-republicans-introduced-916-bills-against-womens-right-to-choose/>

"Group Cites Grim Status of Afghan Women." Arizona Daily Star 30 May 2005:A1.

"H5N1." Wikipedia. 17 May 12 < http://en.wikipedia.org/wiki/Avian_influenza>

"How Do Birth Control Pills Work?" 10 May 12. Go Ask Alice. <http://goaskalice.columbia.edu/how-do-birth-control-pills-work>

"Human Population Control." Wikipedia. 25 May 12 <http://en.wikipedia.org/wiki/Human_population_control >

IRWIN, JAMES B. [Apollo 15] Great Aviation Quotes. 24 Dec. 2003 <http://

www.skygod.com/cgi/search.pl

"Islamic Family Planning." Epigee. 23 May 12 < http://www.epigee.org/Quide/Islamic.html>

JENNINGS, GEORGE J. "Cultural Factors Affecting Human Fertility.*" 23 May 12 <http://www.asa3.org/ASA/PSCF/1970/JASA6-70Jennings.html>

KENT, JONATHAN. "Bird Flu Experts Warn of Pandemic." BBC News 4 July 2005<http://news.bbc.co.uk/1/hi/world/asia-pacific/4647485.stm>

KIRBY, ALEX. "Europe's Five Worst Child Killers." BBC News. 18 June 2004 <http://news.bbc.co.uk/1/hi/sci/tech/3816579.stm

_____ "Fossil Fuel Subsidies 'Must End.'" BBC News 21 June 2004 <http://news.bbc.co.uk/1/hi/sci/tech/38189995.stm>

_____ "Global Sewage Torrent Harms Young." BBC News. 24 June 2004<http://news.bbc.co.uk/1/hi/sci/tech/3832329>

_____."World Warned on Water Refugees." BBC News. 4 Mar. 2004<http://newsvote.bbc.co.uk/1/low/sci/tech/1234244.stm>

KNOX, NOELLE. "Nordic Family Ties Don't Mean Tying the Knot." USA Today 16

Dec. 2004: 15A-16A.

KNOX, RICHARD. "Fewer Boys Being Born in America." Morning Edition. NPR.KUAZ. Tucson. 21 June 2005.

KOPP, DR. BRIAN. "Protestants and Birth Control." Free Public. 09 Jun 10. 23 May 12 <http://www.freepublic.com/f-religion/2531431/posts>

"Love's Strange Effect on People." BBC News. 6 May 2004 <http://news.bbc.co.uk/1/hi/health/3685713.stm>

LOWEN, LINDA. "Majority of WomenWho Terminate a Pregnancy Cite One of Three Reasons." 09 Jun 12 <http://womensissues.about.con/od/reproductiverights/a/Abortion Reasons.html>

MEAD, MARGARET. 31 May 2004 <http://xplore.com/quotes/authors/m/margaret_mead.html>

MEADOWS, DONELLA, JORGEN RANDERS, AND DENNIS MEADOWS. "A Synopsis: Limits to Growth—The 20-Year update." The Reporter Spring 2005: 30-39.

"Measures of Differences." News Night with Aaron Brown. CNN. Tucson.14 Feb. 2005.

MILLER, STEPHEN. "Gaia Hypothesis." Rev. of *The Ages of Gaia* by James Lovelock. 14 June 2004 <http://erg.ucd.ie/arupa/references/gaia.html>

MORGAN, ELAINE. *The Descent of Woman*. New York: Stein and Day, 1972.

"Mormonism." Wikipedia. <http://en.wikipedia.org/wiki/Christian_views_on_contraception>

"Morning-After Pill." Mayo Clinic. 19 May 12
<http://www.Mayoclinic.com/health/morning-after-pill/myo11907>

"The Most Deadly 100 Natural Disasters of the 20th Century."
Disaster Center.17 Mar. 2005
<http://www.disastercenter.com/disaster/TOP100K.html>

"Mother Heroine." Wikipedia. 26 May 12
<http://en.wikipedia.org/wiki/Mother_Hero>

My Fair Lady. Dir. George Cukor. With Rex Harrison and Audrey Hepburn.

Warner Bros. 1964.

"A New Kind of Diaphragm." PATH. 02 Jun 12
<http://www.path.org/projects/si/es.phpSingle-sized>

"New Sinple Methods of Natural Family Planning." 02 Jun 12
<http://archive.irh.org/nfp.htm>

OLSON, WALTER. "Free to Commit." Reason Oct. 1997. 26
Dec. 2004 <http://reason.com/9710/col.olson.shtml>

"On the Status of the Sexes." USA Today 3 Feb. 2005: 12.

'"One-Stop" Embryo Test Unveiled.' BBC News. 24 Oct 08. 07
Jun 12 <http://news.bbc.co.uk/go/pr/fr/_/2/hi/health/7688299.stm>

PILKINGTON, ED. "US Set for Dramatic Change as White
America Becomes Minority by 2042."The Guardian. 08 Jun 12
<http://www.guardian.com.uk/world/2998/aug/15/population.race
>

"Population Control in Singapore." Wikipedia. 25 May 12
<http://en.wikipedia.org/wiki/Family_planning_in_Singapore>

QUIJANO NV, JR. "Herbal Contraceptives: Exploring Indigenous
Methods of Family Planning." 02 Jun 12 <
http://www.ncbi.nlm.nih.gov/pubmed/12280742>

RAGHAVEN, SUDARSAN. "Afghan Girl Given as Bride at 9, Fights for Divorce." Arizona Daily Star 14 Nov. 2004: A15.

REAGAN, LESLIE J. *When Abortion Was a Crime*. Los Angeles: University of California Press, 1997. 1-18.

RICE, AARON. "The Black Death: Bubonic Plague" 8 Dec. 1994. 10 Apr. 2004 <http://www.byu.edu/isp/projects/middleages/LifeTimes/Plague.html

RICHARDS, CECILE AND WIRTH, TIMOTHY E. "Committee Hears Impacts of Ab-Only." 25 Apr 08. 08 Jun 12 <http://www.rhrealitycheck.org/blog/2008/04/24/congressional-committee-hear-impacts-of-ab-only>

"Roman Catholicism." Wikipedia. 23 May 2012 <http://en.wikipedia.org/wiki/Christian_views_on_contraception>

ROSS, MICHAEL. "Sex in America." Psychology Today" 09 Jun 12 <http://www.psychologytoday.com/200201/sex-in-america>

ROSS, STEVEN L. "Abortion and the Death of the Fetus." *Moral Issues*. (Ed) Jan Narveson. New York: Oxford UP. 1983, 239-49.

"Rwanda: A Brief History of Events." Hotel Rwanda. 29 June 2005 <http://hotelrwanda.com/main.html

"Science of the Sexes: 2. Different by Design." The Discovery Channel. DVD: 2003.

SHLAIN, LEONARD. *Sex, Time and Power: How Women's Sexuality Shaped Human Evolution.* New York: Viking, 2003.

SIMON, PAUL. "Citizen of the Planet." 14 June 2004 <http://www.wbr.com/paulsimon/lyrics/citizen_of_the_planet.htm>

SINGER, PETER. *Writings on an Ethical Life*. New York: Harper, 2000.

"Source List and Detailed Death Tolls for the Primary Megadeaths of the Twentieth Century." 30 Jun 12
<http://necrometrics.com/20c5m.htm>

STANTON, GLENN T. "Fact Sheet on Divorce in America." Smart Marriages. 16

Dec. 2004 <http://www.smartmarriages.com/divorce_brief.html>

"Storm Cost 'Could Rise by 66%.'" BBC News. 29 June 2005
<http://news.bbc.co.uk/1/hi/business/4631283.stm>

"Study: Marriage produces More Stable Family." Arizona Daily Star 25 Dec. 2003: A2.

"Sustainability: Considering Lessons from History." Background Information, 8 Oct. 2004
<http://www.aces.uiuc.edu/~sare/backinfo.html>

"Table 2." All Races, Percent Childless. 10 May 12
<http:www.census.gov/hhe/fertility>

"Three Billion More." NOVA. 17 Jan. 2005
<http://www.pbs.org/wgbh/nova/worldbalance/voic-brow.html>

"Title X Family Planning." 26 May 12
<http://www.hhs.gov/org/title-x-family-planning>

"Tsunami Aid 'Went to the Richest.'" BBC News. 25 June 2005
<http://news.bbc.co.uk/1/hi/world/south_asia/4621365.stm>

"Universal Declaration of Human Rights." BBC World Service. 22 Dec. 2003

<http://www.bbc.co.uk/worldservice/people/features/havearightto/four_b/full_text.shtml>

VERGANO, DAN. "Water Shortages Will Leave World in Dire Straits." USA Today. 4 May 2004
<http://www.usatoday.com/news/nation/2003-01-26-water-usat_x.htm>

WALKER, ALICE. "We Have a Beautiful Mother" 1991. *The Oxford Dictionary of Phrase, Saying, and Quotation.* (Ed.) Elizabeth Knowles. New York: Oxford UP, 1997.

WHITEHOUSE, DAVID. "Half of Humanity Set to Go Urban." BBC News. 20 May 2005 <http://news.bbc.co.uk/1/hi/sci/tech/4561183.stm>

WILSON, KELPIE. "Abortion and the Earth." 29 Jan 08. 29 Jun 12 <http://www.kelpiewilson.com/patriarchy>

"Women's Health." 09 Jun 12 <http://women.webmd.com/tc/abortion-reasons-women-choose-abortion>

"World AIDS and HIV Statistics." Avert. 27 June 2005 <http://www.avert.org/worldstats.htm>

"World Divorce Statistics." 07 May 1 <http://www.divorcemag.com/statistics/statsWorld.shtml>

"World Faces Seeping Flood Crisis." BBC News. 14 June 2004 <http://news.bbc.co.uk/1/hi/sci/tech/3803648.stm>

WRIGHT, ROBERT. "Up from Gorilla Land: The Hidden Logic of Love and Lust." Psychology Today. Mar/Apr.1995. 10 July 2003 <http://www.psychologytoday.com/htdocs/prod/ptoarticle/pto-19950301-000023.asp>

###

Who Controls?

www.ingramcontent.com/pod-product-compliance
Lightning Source LLC
Chambersburg PA
CBHW072323290526
45794CB00002B/735